Federal Budget Policy

FEDERAL BUDGET POLICY
Third Edition

David J. Ott and Attiat F. Ott

Decisions about federal spending and taxes are critical not only for the economy and national defense but also for the individual citizen since they affect the availability of jobs and the value of the dollar. The purpose of this book is to provide the general reader with a basis for making informed judgments about federal fiscal programs and policies. It describes and analyzes the history of federal expenditure and tax policy, the budget process, and the budget concepts that have been used to report federal fiscal activity. This revised edition, the seventh in the second series of Studies of Government Finance, includes discussion of the new procedures carried out by the budget committees in the Senate and the House and by the Congressional Budget Office.

Comments on earlier editions:

"Its greatest strength lies in the author's ability to be both concise and clear while explaining a most complicated economic institution — the federal budget." *Annals.*

"... provides a simple account of the main issues involved in controlling the economy...without indulging in unnecessary technicalities." *International Affairs.*

"It has a place on the shelf of most any college library." *Choice.*

Attiat F. Ott is professor of economics at Clark University and a member of the Brookings associated staff. The late David J. Ott was co-author of another Brookings study, *Federal Tax Treatment of State and Local Securities.*

Studies of Government Finance: Second Series

TITLES PUBLISHED

Federal Budget Policy

DAVID J. OTT
and ATTIAT F. OTT

THIRD EDITION

Studies of Government Finance

THE BROOKINGS INSTITUTION

WASHINGTON, D.C.

Library of Congress Cataloging in Publication Data:

Ott, David J
  Federal budget policy.
  (Studies in government finance; 2d ser., book 7)
  Bibliography: p.
  Includes index.
  1. Budget—United States. 2. Fiscal policy—
United States. I. Ott, Attiat F., joint author.
II. Title. III. Series.
HJ2052.08 1977   353.007'22   77-24198
ISBN 0-8157-6710-2
ISBN 0-8157-6709-0 pbk.

In memory of
my husband and coauthor
DAVID JACKSON OTT
A.F.O.

THE BROOKINGS INSTITUTION is an independent organization devoted to nonpartisan research, education, and publication in economics, government, foreign policy, and the social sciences generally. Its principal purposes are to aid in the development of sound public policies and to promote public understanding of issues of national importance.

The Institution was founded on December 8, 1927, to merge the activities of the Institute for Government Research, founded in 1916, the Institute of Economics, founded in 1922, and the Robert Brookings Graduate School of Economics and Government, founded in 1924.

The Board of Trustees is responsible for the general administration of the Institution, while the immediate direction of the policies, program, and staff is vested in the President, assisted by an advisory committee of the officers and staff. The by-laws of the Institution state: "It is the function of the Trustees to make possible the conduct of scientific research, and publication, under the most favorable conditions, and to safeguard the independence of the research staff in the pursuit of their studies and in the publication of the results of such studies. It is not a part of their function to determine, control, or influence the conduct of particular investigations or the conclusions reached."

The President bears final responsibility for the decision to publish a manuscript as a Brookings book. In reaching his judgment on the competence, accuracy, and objectivity of each study, the President is advised by the director of the appropriate research program and weighs the views of a panel of expert outside readers who report to him in confidence on the quality of the work. Publication of a work signifies that it is deemed a competent treatment worthy of public consideration but does not imply endorsement of conclusions or recommendations.

The Institution maintains its position of neutrality on issues of public policy in order to safeguard the intellectual freedom of the staff. Hence interpretations or conclusions in Brookings publications should be understood to be solely those of the authors and should not be attributed to the Institution, to its trustees, officers, or other staff members, or to the organizations that support its research.

Foreword

THE FEDERAL BUDGET is important to every citizen. It is the basic
planning document of the federal government, and at all times it
exerts a significant influence on the state of the economy. It reflects
the President's priorities and his proposals to vary outlays and taxes
to promote economic stability and growth. The annual review of the
budget gives Congress the opportunity to evaluate the effectiveness
of federal programs and to endorse or modify the President's
proposals.

The purpose of this book is to help the nontechnical reader understand the budget and how budget decisions are made. It traces the
history of federal expenditures, taxes, and the national debt, describes
the budget process and explains the concepts used in the budget,
analyzes the effect of fiscal policy on economic activity, and discusses
methods of determining the appropriate level of federal expenditures.
Together with its companion volumes, James A. Maxwell's *Financing State and Local Governments* and Joseph A. Pechman's *Federal
Tax Policy*, it presents the accumulated knowledge of economists
and others about government finance so as to sharpen public per-
ception of the issues and to make factual and institutional materials
easily available.

The third edition of this book was prepared by Attiat F. Ott, professor of economics at Clark University and a member of the associated staff of the Brookings Institution. She is grateful to Dan Larkins of the American Enterprise Institute for Public Policy Research, who prepared a first draft of the revision of chapters 2 and 4; to the staff of the Office of Management and Budget, especially Carey P. Modlin, Robert Kilpatrick, and Roselee Roberts, for comments helpful in revising chapter 3; to Russell Cooper and Jared Lobdell of Clark University; and to Robert W. Hartman, Charles L. Schultze, and Emil M. Sunley, Jr., of the Brookings staff, for criticism and suggestions that improved the manuscript in many ways. The manuscript was edited by Ellen Alston and reviewed for accuracy by Evelyn P. Fisher. The index was prepared by Brian Svikhart; the charts, by the Ford Studios. The project was carried out as part of the Brookings Economic Studies program, which is directed by Joseph A. Pechman.

David J. Ott died in May 1975, before the work on this revision was completed. The loss is especially painful for those who were associated with him in the field of public finance, to which he made many scholarly contributions.

This is the seventh publication in the second series of Brookings Studies of Government Finance, which is devoted to examining issues in taxation and public expenditure policy. The authors' views are their own and should not be attributed to the trustees, officers, or other staff members of the Brookings Institution.

BRUCE K. MAC LAURY
President

June 1977
Washington, D.C.

Contents

Text Tables

Appendix Tables

Figures

CHAPTER ONE

Introduction

THE FEDERAL BUDGET of the United States amounts to one-fifth of the total national output, or gross national product. Decisions on taxes and expenditures affect jobs, the "value of the dollar," the growth of the economy, and national defense. They bear on the questions of government versus private use of resources, federal versus state and local government responsibilities, and the viability of the private enterprise economy.

Those who make the critical decisions on these matters rely on staff specialists as well as on their own knowledge and experience. But the layman, who must ultimately judge the wisdom of the decisions, often lacks any basis for informed judgment. To be informed about budget policy requires some familiarity with budget accounting concepts, the budget process, and the history of federal budget experience. To make informed judgments about federal spending and tax policy requires knowledge of what the budget *should* do. This is true both for the President and his staff, who formulate federal budget policy, and for the congressman and the individual citizen, who must judge the President's fiscal program.

The purposes of this volume are first, to explain (as far as possible in nontechnical language) the criteria that most economists would offer to guide decisions about federal spending and taxation, and

1

second, to provide institutional and descriptive material about the federal budget, federal budgeting history, and how the budget is formulated, in order to help the reader understand current budget policies.

The book begins with factual and descriptive background material. Chapter 2 explains the ways in which federal fiscal activity may be reported and the uses and limitations of each concept of the federal budget. Particular attention is given to the differences between the three most commonly used budgets—the unified budget, the national income budget, and the full- or high-employment budget. Chapter 3 tells how the federal budget is made, from the formulation and presentation of the President's budget through congressional consideration and approval, the actual disbursement of funds, and the audit of accounts. This chapter also summarizes past improvements in the budget process and discusses in detail the new Congressional Budget and Impoundment Control Act of 1974. Chapter 4 reviews the history of federal finance since the early 1790s, including trends in federal expenditures relative to output, population, and prices and in the composition of federal expenditures. Changes in the types of receipts are also discussed, together with the record of deficits and surpluses.

The impact of budget policy on the nation's economy is discussed in chapter 5. It explains how tax and expenditure decisions of the federal government affect output, employment, and prices and how budget policy together with monetary policy can help achieve certain economic goals related to output, employment, and prices. The practical problems involved in using the budget as an instrument to affect the economy are given special atttention in chapter 6, along with possible alternative budget programs. The stabilizing budget proposal of the Committee for Economic Development and the Swedish budget proposals are also discussed here.

If the budget policy of the federal government requires deficits and an increase in the national debt, what will be the results? Is there a burden associated with the national debt? Will increases in the national debt lead to bankruptcy? These and other issues are taken up in chapter 7. The final chapter deals with criteria for judging federal spending—both the total amount and the amount for each function—apart from its impact on output, prices, and employment.

The reader should remember that expenditure and tax policy is not only important, it is also controversial. An administration's budget policy is often the leading domestic issue in national elections. This increases the public's need to be informed on the facts and significance of budget decisions, but it makes a completely objective study of budget policy difficult, particularly since economists themselves disagree on various aspects of budget policy. One of the objectives of this volume is to present the views dominant among professional economists about budget policy and to indicate areas where disagreement exists.

CHAPTER TWO

The Federal Budget: Concepts and Uses

FEDERAL FISCAL ACTIVITY can be reported in a number of ways. In this chapter several of the most important are examined, with emphasis on the advantages and disadvantages of each.

The Unified Federal Budget

Before fiscal year 1969, the President's budget emphasized different budget concepts in different years, with resulting confusion among the news media in their attempts to report on it, among congressmen in public statements and congressional debate, and certainly among the citizenry in discussing and evaluating federal budget policy. Charges of "gimmickry" were leveled at the federal government from time to time when there were changes in the budget concepts being used.

In the midst of growing public concern over the citizen's ability to understand and evaluate federal budget policy, President Lyndon B. Johnson appointed the President's Commission on Budget Concepts in March 1967 to make a thorough study of the federal budget and the problems of presenting it to the Congress and the public and to make recommendations. The report of the commission (in October 1967) suggested a budget format that would reduce confusion but at the same time provide the necessary information for decisions on fiscal policy that affect the level of economic activity and for decisions on the allocation of resources among federal government programs.[1] This proposal was substantially adopted as the official format beginning with the fiscal year 1969 budget (presented in January 1968). Since that time, however, the format has undergone several changes, and it now differs in several important respects from the original recommendation. The following section identifies these differences and assesses their significance.

Table 2-1 presents a summary of the budget for fiscal year 1976, compiled from data that appear in the 1978 budget document. The budget presentations now are both more comprehensive and better integrated than those used before the adoption of the unified budget. (Detailed supplementary budget tables for various years are given in appendix A.)

The first section of the table reports on budget authority for the 1976 fiscal year. Budget authority, granted by Congress, confers on the government the right to incur financial obligations. The table shows that $201.7 billion of budget authority was available in fiscal year 1976 as a result of earlier congressional actions; $266.9 billion of the proposed authority required current action by Congress. "Deductions for offsetting receipts" arise for two reasons. First, budget receipts of government enterprises are treated as offsets to expenditures (negative expenditures) if the activity generating the receipts is market-oriented as opposed to being essentially a government activity—that is, one involving compulsion or regulation. Thus, the receipts of the Tennessee Valley Authority from the sale of electricity are counted as expenditure offsets and enter the budget as negative expenditures, while patent and copyright fees are counted as receipts and not netted out, since they come from a regulatory activity of the government. Second, in order to avoid counting the same transaction twice, transactions between (or among) government agencies must also be netted out. These intragovernmental transactions are also included as offsetting receipts.

The second part of table 2-1 presents receipts, outlays, and the re-

1. *Report of the President's Commission on Budget Concepts* (Government Printing Office, 1967).

Table 2-1. Budget Summary, Fiscal Year 1976

Description	Millions of dollars
Budget authority	
Available through current action by Congress	266,933
Available without current action by Congress	201,724
Deductions for offsetting receipts[a]	− 53,321
Total budget authority	415,336
Receipts, outlays, and surplus or deficit	
Receipts	
Federal funds	201,099
Trust funds	133,695
Interfund transactions	− 34,789
Total budget receipts	300,005
Outlays	
Federal funds	269,969
Trust funds	131,286
Interfund transactions	− 34,789
Total budget outlays	366,466
Surplus or deficit	
Federal funds	− 68,870
Trust funds	2,409
Total budget deficit	− 66,461
Outstanding debt at end of period	
Held by government agencies	151,566
Held by the public	480,300
Gross federal debt	631,866
Memorandum: Outstanding loans at end of year	
Direct loans, on-budget accounts	64,233
Direct loans, off-budget accounts	21,646
Guaranteed and insured loans[b]	169,828
Government-sponsored enterprise loans[c]	84,930

Source: *The Budget of the United States Government, Fiscal Year 1978*, pp. 371, 425, 433.

a. These consist of intragovernmental transactions and proprietary receipts from the public.

b. Excludes loans held by government accounts and sponsored credit enterprises.

c. Net of lendings among government-sponsored enterprises or between such enterprises and federal agencies; excludes Federal Reserve banks.

sulting budget deficit. Receipts earmarked for trust funds (and outlays from trust funds) are distinguished from all other government receipts and outlays (federal funds). By distinguishing between trust funds and federal funds, the summary, in effect, resurrects the old "administrative" budget, frequently used, and justly criticized, in the 1950s and 1960s. (The principal differences between the administrative budget and the unified budget are first, the unified budget includes receipts and outlays of trust funds while the administrative budget does not, and second, the unified budget eliminates inter-agency transactions.) Thus the federal funds deficit shown in table 2-1 is essentially the administrative budget deficit. The Commission on Budget Concepts, however, had recommended "strongly that the President's budget presentation give no attention to a surplus or deficit calculated on the basis of the administrative budget."[2]

The budget summary also differs from what was suggested by the commission in using the single concept "outlays" to denote disbursements of funds. Outlays include net lending by the government as well as government spending. The commission had recommended that net lending be clearly distinguished from expenditures in the budget summary. This recommendation was based on the belief that the economic impact of government lending differs from that of government spending on goods and services and from that of transfer payments such as social security benefits. When the federal government makes a loan, the commission reasoned, the recipient incurs a liability; his spending behavior is thus likely to be different from the spending behavior of a recipient of social security benefits or of a federal wage payment. George F. Break, on the other hand, has argued that the effects of lending and spending are identical, both depending in large measure on the way they are financed.[3] In any event, net lending included in the budget is small in comparison with expenditures and little would be gained by distinguishing the two in the summary table.

A final way in which the second section of table 2-1 differs from the commission's recommendations is found in the time when budgetary aggregates are measured. In the budget, outlays are counted when the government issues checks in payment of its obligations, and receipts are counted when checks are received from taxpayers and others. The commission recommended putting all receipts and expenditures on an accrual basis—that is, counting expenditures when the government incurs a liability to pay for goods and services and counting receipts when the private sector incurs a liability to make payments to the federal government. The logic of this concept is that the economic impact of the budget presumably occurs when goods

2. *Report of the President's Commission on Budget Concepts*, p. 27.
3. George F. Break, *Federal Lending and Economic Stability* (Brookings Institution, 1965), pp. 14–18.

are produced for federal government use and when taxpayers incur a tax liability to the government.

The final line of the second section of table 2-1 presents the overall budget surplus or deficit. It is obtained by adding the surplus or deficit of the trust funds to the surplus or deficit of the federal funds. Typically, outlays of federal funds exceed receipts—that is, there is a deficit in the federal funds accounts—while trust fund outlays are less than receipts, so the trust funds are in surplus.

The third section of table 2-1 shows the effect that the budget deficit had on the federal debt. The public's holdings of government debt at the end of fiscal 1975 were $396.9 billion. The table indicates that the debt increased by $83.4 billion in 1976, to $480.3 billion. How can this be when the deficit is estimated to be "only" $66.5 billion? The answer is shown in the following tabulation:[4]

	Billions of dollars
Budget deficit	66.5
Deficit, off-budget federal entities	7.2
Means of financing other than borrowing from the public	
Increase in cash and monetary assets	8.0
Increase in liabilities	1.3
Total requirements for borrowing from the public	82.9
Increase in debt due to reclassification of securities	0.5
Change in debt held by the public	83.4

In addition to borrowing funds to cover the difference between outlays and receipts, the Treasury Department also borrowed $9.3 billion to increase its cash balances and liabilities. Another half-billion dollars is accounted for by a reclassification of certain Export-Import Bank certificates from asset sales to debt. The remaining part of the discrepancy between the deficit and borrowing from the public is explained in the second line of the tabulation. Not included in the budget outlays of $366 billion and the deficit of $66.5 billion (table 2-1) are about $7.2 billion of outlays—mostly loans that were extended by wholly owned federal agencies or entities and had to be

4. See *The Budget of the United States Government, Fiscal Year 1978*, pp. 371, 379, 425, 433.

financed by federal borrowing from the public.[5] The exclusion of these loans from the budget totals represents perhaps the major difference between the treatment recommended by the President's Commission on Budget Concepts and the procedures actually followed in the unified budget. The commission strongly recommended that "the budget should include all programs of the Federal Government and its agencies."[6]

The off-budget agencies, according to former Assistant Secretary of the Treasury Murray L. Weidenbaum, "possess a unique set of characteristics: (1) They fully meet the coverage tests of the unified budget concept established by the President's Commission on Budget Concepts and (2) they have arbitrarily been moved out of the unified budget by specific congressional statute." He goes on to remind us that "it was precisely budget gimmicks of this nature . . . that led to discrediting the old conventional budget and to its replacement by the unified budget."[7]

The growth in the importance of off-budget agencies, with the corresponding reduction in the significance of the deficit reported in the budget, is reflected in table 2-2. From $1.4 billion dollars in fiscal year 1974, outlays of off-budget agencies reached $8 billion in 1975 and are estimated at $11 billion for fiscal year 1979.

The off-budget and other outstanding loans are shown in the memorandum section of table 2-1. Remaining to be explained are outstanding direct loans of agencies that are included in the budget (first line); government-insured loans outstanding (third line), which represent only contingent liabilities and do not enter into the budget totals; and outstanding direct loans of federally sponsored enterprises (line 4). These federally sponsored agencies were created by the federal government but were later converted to private ownership. Since they are now private corporations, they are excluded from the budget

5. For fiscal year 1976, the list of off-budget agencies is as follows: Postal Service fund, Rural Telephone Bank, housing for the elderly or handicapped fund, Federal Financing Bank, United States Railway Association, Pension Benefit Guaranty Corporation, rural electrification and telephone revolving fund, and exchange stabilization fund.

6. *Report of the President's Commission on Budget Concepts,* p. 7.

7. Murray L. Weidenbaum, "Comments on Teeters' 'Current Problems in the Full Employment Concept,'" *Studies in Price Stability and Economic Growth,* papers 6 and 7, Prepared for the Use of the Joint Economic Committee, 94:1 (GPO, 1975), p. 18.

Table 2-2. Outlays of Off-Budget Federal Entities, in Relation to Total Outlays, 1973–79

Outlays in billions of dollars

Fiscal year	Off-budget outlays	Unified budget outlays	Off-budget as percent of total outlays
1973	0.1	247.1	*
1974	1.4	269.6	0.5
1975	8.0	326.1	2.5
1976	7.2	366.5	2.0
TQ[a]	1.8	94.7	1.9
1977[b]	10.8	411.2	2.6
1978[b]	9.2	440.0	2.1
1979[b]	10.9	466.0	2.3

Source: *The Budget of the United States Government, Fiscal Year 1978*, p. 26.
* Less than 0.05.
a. Transition quarter.
b. Estimate.

totals, in accordance with the recommendations of the Commission on Budget Concepts.[8]

A Comparison of the Unified Budget and Other Budget Concepts

Two important budget concepts occur frequently in discussions of fiscal policy—the national income accounts budget and the full- or high-employment budget. The budget in the national income accounts is considered first.

The Federal Sector of the National Income Accounts

The federal sector of the national income accounts, or the national income accounts budget (as it is often called), corresponds in concept to the system followed in the national income accounts—a system of dual-entry accounts used by the Department of Commerce to estimate the current productive activity of residents of the United States. On one side, the accounts show the market values of the currently produced output of goods and services, classified by type of

8. The list of federally sponsored agencies is as follows: Federal National Mortgage Association, Student Loan Marketing Association, the Farm Credit System (including banks for cooperatives, federal intermediate credit banks, and federal land banks), and the Federal Home Loan Bank System (composed of federal home loan banks and the Federal Home Loan Mortgage Corporation).

expenditure—consumer expenditures, gross private expenditures on equipment, new construction, inventories, federal, state, and local government purchases of goods and services, and net exports. The total of these items is called the gross national product (GNP). On the other side, the accounts measure and classify the stream of income generated in the process of producing GNP: wages and salaries, professional income, rental income, corporate profits, and interest.

The federal sector of the national income accounts differs from receipts and outlays in the unified budget principally in three respects. First, the timing of receipts and expenditures is different in the two budgets. In the unified budget, receipts are counted when the cash is collected and most expenditures are counted when checks are issued (except interest, which is recorded when it accrues). In the national income accounts (NIA) budget, on the other hand, receipts (except for nonwithheld personal taxes) are reported on an accrual basis (when income is earned or when a liability to pay the federal government is incurred), but expenditures are reported in several ways—on an accrual basis for construction and interest outlays, on a "delivery" basis for other goods purchased, and on a checks-issued basis for grants-in-aid, subsidies, and transfer payments. An adjustment must therefore be made in order to reconcile the differences in the timing of receipts and expenditures in the two budgets.

Second, both receipts and outlays in the NIA budget are increased by the amount of the government's contributions to its employee retirement plans because these amounts are counted as part of the compensation of employees. (These payments by the government to itself are netted out in the unified budget.) And finally, net lending is excluded from NIA outlays because it represents an exchange of one asset for another, rather than an expenditure for currently produced goods and services. Table 2-3 shows the overall relation between receipts and outlays of the unified budget and the NIA budget.

Why bother to develop an NIA budget? The answer is that, by eliminating such things as purely financial transactions (those involving the exchange of assets) and by using the accrual method, the NIA budget provides a better measure of the impact of fiscal policy than does the unified budget. True, in fiscal year 1976 converting from the unified to the NIA budget made relatively little difference in the deficit: the unified budget shows a deficit of $66.5 billion compared with the NIA budget deficit of $59.4 billion.

Table 2-3. Relation of the Unified Budget to the National Income Accounts Budget, Fiscal Year 1976

Description	Billions of dollars
Unified budget receipts	300.0
Plus: Government contribution for employee retirement (grossing)	6.0
Other netting and grossing	2.3
Adjustment to accruals	6.0
Other	−0.8
Equals: National income accounts receipts	313.6
Unified budget outlays	366.5
Plus: Lending and financial transactions	−4.8
Government contribution for employee retirement (grossing)	6.0
Other netting and grossing	2.3
Defense timing adjustment	2.6
Bonuses on outer continental shelf land leases	2.1
Other	−1.7
Equals: National income accounts expenditures	373.0

Source: *Special Analyses, Budget of the United States Government, Fiscal Year 1978*, p. 24.

But the two measures are not always so close. In fiscal year 1968, for example, the exclusion of $6 billion in loans from the NIA budget, and the inclusion of more than $4 billion in receipts as a result of adjusting receipts to an accrual basis, produced an NIA budget deficit only about half the size of the unified budget deficit of $25 billion. In fact, the two deficits have usually been within a few billion dollars of each other over the past dozen years or so; occasionally, however, the NIA and unified budgets differ substantially.

A further reason for preferring the NIA to the unified budget is the need for consistency when comparing data. Economists typically use the gross national product, or some variant thereof, as an indicator of the level of economic activity. To see how government affects the level of economic activity, it is desirable to use as a measure of government policy a series that is conceptually consistent with the GNP estimates. The NIA budget does correspond to the system used to measure GNP while the unified budget does not.

The Full-Employment Budget

Federal receipts and outlays are not determined solely by tax laws and appropriations bills. They are also determined in part by the level of economic activity. When the economy enters a recession, for example, and incomes, both corporate and personal, fall, the level of tax receipts falls and (as discussed in detail in chapter 6) this exerts an automatic stabilizing influence on the economy. Outlays, on the other hand, rise during the recession as more people become eligible to receive benefits from such programs as unemployment compensation and food stamps.

Thus, in addition to the budget's effects on the economy, the economy has effects on the budget. In order to disentangle the two interacting forces, economists have developed the concept of the full-employment budget. This is a hypothetical construct designed to insulate the budget totals from the effects of changes in the level of economic activity. It shows what outlays and receipts would be if the labor force were fully employed.[9] Table 2-4 shows the relationship between the full-employment budget and the NIA budget.[10]

The NIA budget deficit of $59 billion for fiscal year 1976 is almost entirely the result of the depressed state of the economy. If the economy had been operating at full employment, the budget would have had a deficit of $8 billion in fiscal year 1976.

To summarize this discussion of commonly used budget concepts, figure 2-1 shows the surplus or deficit for the unified budget, the NIA budget, and the full-employment budget for fiscal years 1956–76.

Tax Expenditures

Outlays are not the only instrument of public policy affecting the economy. Statutes such as the antitrust and environmental laws have significant effects, and the impact of governmental regulatory agencies goes far beyond what one might guess just from looking at the outlays of those agencies in the budget. These effects, however, are extrabudgetary and, in any case, are widely known; it would be both inappropriate and unnecessary to dwell on them here. "Tax expendi-

9. From the early 1960s, an unemployment rate of 4 percent was used to define a condition of full employment, although this definition was frequently criticized, especially in the 1970s. In its 1977 annual report, the Council of Economic Advisers suggested a 4.9 rate as more appropriate to take account of changes in the composition of the labor force since the mid-1950s. Figure 2-1 incorporates a full-employment unemployment rate that varies from 4 percent in calendar year 1955 to 4.9 percent in 1976.

10. Both the unified budget and the NIA budget can be converted to full-employment budgets. Since the full-employment budget is designed to facilitate economic analysis of fiscal policy, however, and since the NIA budget is the one most commonly used for evaluating the economic effects of budget policy, table 2-4 shows only how the NIA budget is adjusted.

Figure 2-1. Federal Deficits and Surpluses under Three Budget Concepts, Fiscal Years 1956–76

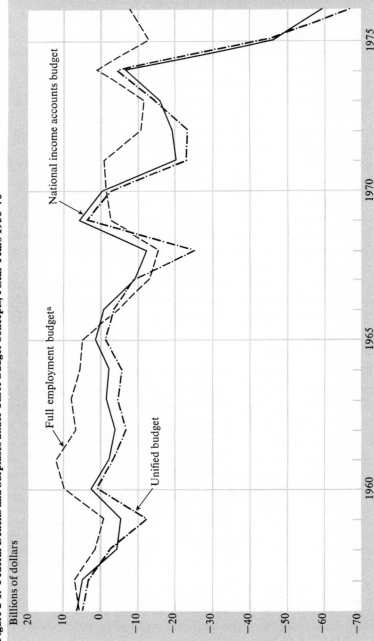

Billions of dollars

Sources: Same as table A-8.

a. National income accounts basis. The calculations assume a full-employment unemployment rate that varies from 4 percent in calendar year 1955 to 4.9 percent in 1976.

Table 2-4. Relation between National Income Accounts and Full-Employment Budget Totals, Fiscal Year 1976[a]

Description	Billions of dollars
National income accounts receipts	313.6
Plus: Adjustment for tax receipts due to deviation of economy from full employment	43.4
Equals: Full-employment receipts	357.0
National income accounts expenditures	373.0
Less: Adjustment for expenditures due to deviation of economy from full employment (primarily unemployment compensation)	7.7
Equals: Full-employment expenditures	365.3
NIA surplus or deficit	−59.4
Full-employment surplus or deficit	−8.2

Sources: Tables 2-3 and A-8; Joseph A. Pechman, ed., *Setting National Priorities: The 1978 Budget* (Brookings Institution, 1977), table A-1, series B. Figures are rounded.

a. The calculations assume a full-employment unemployment rate of 4.9 percent.

tures"—another instrument of public policy—however, are not so well understood.

Tax expenditures are, in effect, subsidies provided by the government through the tax system to encourage certain activities and to assist certain groups. For example, capital formation is encouraged by permitting businesses to claim some portion of the cost of an investment as a credit on its income tax, and the unemployed are aided by excluding unemployment benefits from taxable income. As is clear from these two examples, tax expenditures involve no transfer of funds from the government to the private sector: the government does not send a check to a business firm, for example, to reimburse it for a portion of its capital investment. Rather, the Treasury Department forgoes some of the revenue that it otherwise would have collected, and the beneficiary taxpayers (including firms) pay lower taxes than they otherwise would have.

Tax expenditures may be defined more formally as those revenue losses attributable to provisions of the federal income tax laws that allow a "special exclusion, exemption, or deduction from gross income or [which provide] a special credit, preferential tax rate, or deferral of tax liability."[11] Provisions resulting in tax expenditures have also been defined as exceptions to the normal structure of the tax system.

11. *The Budget of the United States Government, Fiscal Year 1978*, p. 34.

**Table 2-5. Estimated Federal Tax Expenditures,
by Budget Function, Fiscal Year 1977**
Millions of dollars

	Amount of tax expenditure	
Budget function and tax provision	Corpo- rations	Indi- viduals
National defense	...	740
International affairs	1,890	160
Exclusion of income earned abroad	...	160
Deferral of income of domestic international sales corporation	1,420	...
Other	470	...
Natural resources, environment, and energy	2,230	960
Exclusion of interest on state and local government pollution control bonds	170	75
Excess of percentage over cost depletion	1,020	575
Other	1,040	310
Agriculture	610	925
Expensing of capital outlays	115	360
Cooperatives: deductibility of noncash patronage dividends and other items	455	...
Capital gains treatment of certain income	40	565
Commerce and transportation	19,670	28,175
Corporate surtax exemption	6,185	...
Deductibility of nonbusiness state gasoline tax	...	600
Investment credit	7,585	1,530
Asset depreciation range	1,630	175
Capital gains: individuals (other than farming or timber)	...	6,225
Capital gains at death	...	7,280
Deductibility of mortgage interest on owner-occupied homes	...	4,710
Deductibility of property tax on owner-occupied homes	...	3,825
Other	4,270	3,830
Community and regional development	25	40
Education, manpower, and social services	647	4,979
Deductibility of charitable contributions (social services)	352	3,124
Other	295	1,855
Health	173	7,151
Income security	...	24,435
Exclusion of social security benefits	...	4,460
Exclusion of unemployment insurance benefits	...	2,855
Net exclusion of pension contributions and earnings	...	7,440
Excess of percentage standard deduction over minimum	...	1,560
Additional exemptions for over 65 and blind	...	1,245
Earned income credit (refundable portion)	...	1,110
Exclusion of interest on life insurance savings	...	1,855
Other	...	3,910

Table 2-5 (*continued*)

Budget function and tax provision	Amount of tax expenditure	
	Corpo-rations	Indi-viduals
Veterans' benefits and services	...	905
Revenue sharing and general-purpose fiscal assistance	3,435	8,070
Exclusion of interest on general-purpose state and local debt	3,150	1,390
Deductibility of nonbusiness state and local taxes (other than on owner-occupied homes and gasoline)	...	6,680
Exclusion of income earned in U.S. possessions	285	...
General government and deferral of interest on savings bonds	...	750
Total, all tax expenditures[a]	28,680	77,290

Source: Congressional Budget Office, *Budget Options for Fiscal Year 1977: A Report to the Senate and House Committees on the Budget* (GPO, 1976), pp. 384–87.

a. The totals are the mathematical sums of the columns. Individual estimates in this table are based on the assumption that no other changes are made in the tax law. Consequently the aggregate revenue effect will not equal the sum of the revenue effects of the individual items shown.

Unfortunately, these definitions are necessarily somewhat ambiguous. The first does not classify all exclusions, exemptions, or deductions as tax expenditures, but only those that are in some way "special." The second definition suggests that these provisions are "special" in that they represent departures from the "normal" structure of the income tax, but the normal structure is not specified.[12]

This is not the place to go into all the considerations involved in determining which tax provisions should be called tax expenditures and which should not. Suffice it to say that there is general agreement on most of the provisions that qualify as tax expenditures. One representative list is given in table 2-5, which also provides estimates of the amounts by which Treasury revenues would increase if these tax expenditures were eliminated.

Several cautions must be kept in mind in interpreting the data. First, and perhaps most important, each estimate is based on the assumption that a particular tax expenditure is eliminated while all the others are retained. Thus the figures in the table are not additive —that is, if two or more tax expenditures were eliminated simul-

12. Congressional Budget Office, *Budget Options for Fiscal Year 1977: A Report to the Senate and House Committees on the Budget* (GPO, 1976), p. 381. See also Senate Committee on the Budget, *Tax Expenditures: Compendium of Background Material on Individual Provisions,* 94:2 (GPO, 1976).

taneously, the resulting revenue gain to the Treasury might be either greater or less than the simple sum of the two items. The reasons are fairly easy to see. If, for example, the deductibility of mortgage interest payments and property taxes were both eliminated, many taxpayers who now itemize their deductions would shift to the standard deduction. Thus the Treasury's gain would be less than the $8.5 billion obtained by adding these two items in the table. On the other hand, if interest on state and local securities were made taxable and if capital gains were treated as ordinary income, many taxpayers would be pushed into higher tax brackets and Treasury receipts would rise by more than the $4.5 billion indicated in the table for tax-exempt interest, all other things being equal.

Second, the benefits of these tax expenditures do not accrue solely to the individual taxpayer directly affected. For example, the deductibility of charitable contributions benefits not only the individual or corporation making the contribution, but also the people and institutions receiving the contributions.

To provide some perspective, the tax expenditure items listed in the table are totaled. The estimated effect of all tax expenditures for fiscal 1977 is $106 billion; of this total, $77 billion benefits individuals, while the remaining $29 billion goes to corporations.

The Congressional Budget Office has also estimated the effect of the President's tax proposals for the 1977 budget on the level of tax expenditures.[13] If enacted, the proposed tax changes would decrease tax expenditures for fiscal year 1977 by about $1,910 million for individuals but increase them by $3,605 million for corporations.

The Capital or Divided Budget

From time to time, proposals have been made that the federal government should adopt another method in presenting its budget—the capital or divided budget. The basic idea of the capital budget is separation of the budget into two parts, the "current" and the "capital" accounts. The general format of a divided budget is shown in

13. *Budget Options for Fiscal Year 1977*, p. 390. The most significant proposals were the replacement of the low-income allowance and the percentage standard deduction with a flat standard deduction, and the expiration of the earned income credit.

Table 2-6. Illustration of a Capital Budget
Billions of dollars

Expenditures		Receipts	
Current account			
Purchases of current goods and services	130	Corporation income tax	80
Transfer payments	50	Individual income tax	120
Grants-in-aid to state and local governments	40	Other	40
Depreciation on government assets	40		
Total	260	Total	240
		Deficit in current account −20	
Capital account			
Purchases of government assets	100	Sales of government assets	10
		Transfer from current account for depreciation	40
Total	100	Total	50
		Deficit in capital account −50	
		Capital budget deficit −70	

table 2-6 with hypothetical dollar entries. The current account shows all expenditures except purchases of assets by the government and all receipts except sales of government assets or government borrowing. The capital account shows purchases of government assets as expenditures and sales of government assets and funds transferred from the current account to cover depreciation as receipts. The budget presented this way shows a deficit of $20 billion in the current account and $50 billion in the capital account.

The capital budget proposal is quite controversial, having perhaps more adversaries than advocates. Briefly, the idea of a capital budget centers on one fundamental concept—government outlays of an investment type should be financed by borrowing while all other outlays should be financed by current taxation. The idea is appealing, although its feasibility and its applicability to the federal budget may be questionable. Advocates of a capital budget argue that it would eliminate the often involved and cumbersome discussion of the burden of the public debt. In addition, the distortion of consumer choice through time caused by debt rather than tax finance of government spending would be eliminated. On the other hand, its critics argue that a capital budget would distort the setting of priorities in government programs, frustrate stabilization policy, and raise a host of problems in its implementation. Before turning to these criticisms, let us first consider the merits of the capital budget as they relate to the burdens and distortions created by debt financing.

As will be seen (in chapter 7), in a full-employment setting, debt-financed public expenditures may impose a "burden" on future generations, either because government borrowing displaces private borrowing and thus reduces private capital formation or because government use of resources through borrowing results in extra taxation imposed on future generations to service the debt. (This debt service has no counterpart when the resource is transferred through taxation.) If a capital budget were adopted, only outlays of the investment type would be financed by debt issues. Since future generations must be expected to benefit from these outlays, no burden would be imposed on them as taxes were increased to service the debt. In this case the capital budget would balance future taxes with future benefits.

The distortion of individuals' choice through time under debt finance occurs because individuals have less than perfect foresight about the relation of their future tax liability (connected with servicing the debt) to their current tax liability. In effect, they shift the burden of the debt-financed outlays to future generations, while no such shift is possible with current taxation. Thus, under conditions of full employment, individuals are able to increase their total consumption (including consumption of government goods and services) through debt finance. Future consumption will be reduced not only because of the lower levels of private capital formation, but also because of the additional future taxes that must be levied to service the debt. On the other hand, if debt finance is restricted to investment-type activities of the federal government, this distortion will not take place—current benefits of government expenditures will be paid for by current taxes and future benefits by future taxes.

The arguments against the capital budget were summed up by Kermit Gordon, who pointed out the inappropriateness of using the capital budgeting concept at the federal level of government for two major reasons. First, unlike the budgets of business firms, the purpose of the federal budget is not to measure profit or show the ownership of assets; rather it is to present in detail the financial dimensions of the President's plan for conducting the affairs of the nation and to show how and to what degree his budget affects aggregate demand in the economy. Exclusion of capital-type outlays from the President's budget would produce confusion rather than clarity. Second, implicit in the "standard" capital budget proposals is the fiscal principle of balancing the ordinary budget and borrowing to finance capital outlays. This system would introduce biases in favor of "investment in bricks and concrete" and against that for "people and knowledge" and does not guarantee a level of aggregate demand consistent with stabilization purposes.[14]

Unquestionably, these criticisms are of great merit. The problem with the capital budget, as this critique implies, does not, however, stem from the concept per se but rather from the "standard" conception of a capital budget.

The adoption of a capital budget bears no relation to what is included in the budget. Under present practice, the federal budget focuses on the President's program rather than on the way the expenditures are financed. Capital budgeting would provide a statement of the sources of funds used to finance government outlays, but it need not supplant the figures now presented in the budget. With respect to the second criticism, the preference for investment in bricks instead of humans need not arise. Government investments in human capital are just as "legitimate" as investments in physical capital. While it would not be easy to separate government outlays on human resources between consumption and investment, it would be desirable to make a start in this direction. Such a breakdown would help to offset the bias against government investments in human capital; it might also lead to modification of other government practices (such as the disallowance for tax purposes of depreciation on human capital and the nondeductibility of educational expenses) that discriminate against private investment in human capital.[15]

Assuming that decisions on government investment policies are part of the budget decisionmaking process, the capital budget would raise three questions. (a) Given the state of the economy, what is the appropriate tax, money, or debt policy? (b) Do the benefits of the project accrue to present as well as future generations or do they only benefit future generations? (c) Are the benefits and costs identifiable and unambiguous?[16] The answers to these questions would be helpful

14. Kermit Gordon, "Reflections on Spending," *Public Policy,* vol. 15 (1966), pp. 7–9 (Brookings Reprint 125).

15. This is done to some degree in the budget presentation in *Special Analyses, Budget of the United States Government, Fiscal Year 1978,* pp. 65–86.

16. For discussion of the use of the capital budget within the framework, see Martin J. Bailey, "The Optimal Full-Employment Surplus," *Journal of Political Economy,* vol. 80 (July–August 1972), pp. 650–53.

in selecting the methods of government finance that are consistent both with stabilization goals and with the objective of matching payments by each generation for the benefits it receives. Suppose that the state of the economy is such that an expansionary fiscal policy is called for. Assume further that the stimulus to the economy provided by debt-financed capital outlays is not sufficient to achieve full employment. In this case, the economy could be further expanded by either increasing the size of the current account budget (an increase in both expenditures and taxes) or by adopting a more expansionary monetary policy to achieve the desired stimulus.[17]

On the other hand, in periods of unemployment, there may be an overriding need to finance current government outlays out of debt in order to stimulate aggregate demand and economic recovery. Tying debt finance to public capital formation may exert an unwarranted constraint on the use of discretionary fiscal policy or could aggravate rather than smooth economic fluctuations if the fall in aggregate demand were temporary.

Thus, the feasibility of capital budgeting hinges on the ability to identify the benefits and beneficiaries of investment projects, and its effect on countercyclical fiscal policy. Until now the concept of capital budgeting for the federal government has been rejected, which suggests that policymakers and budget experts believe that a capital budget would be difficult to implement and might also hinder the use of budget policy for stabilization purposes.

Summary

Three different budget concepts, each with its own particular uses, have been examined in this chapter. The unified budget proposed by the President and modified and enacted by the Congress is the financial plan of the federal government. The NIA budget, which is a statement of federal spending and taxation as recorded in the national income accounts, measures the impact of fiscal policy on the economy. The full-employment budget is a hypothetical construct designed to show what expenditures and taxes would be if the economy were operating at full employment.

Proposals for a federal capital budget were also examined. The

17. For stabilization policy in the context of a capital budget, great reliance is placed on monetary policy. See ibid.

capital budget would help to identify the government outlays that should be financed by debt, but would probably be difficult to implement. Tax expenditures—that is, subsidies provided by the federal government through the tax system rather than through direct expenditures—were discussed. Estimates of tax expenditures, which are presented regularly in the federal budget document and also appear in reports of the Congressional Budget Office, have focused attention on the efficiency and distributional effects of tax preferences.

CHAPTER THREE

The Budget Process

CRUCIAL to any discussion of budget policy, which entails the setting of levels and composition of taxes and expenditures to achieve certain goals, is an understanding of the administrative and political process through which expenditures and taxes are determined. This chapter describes the process at the federal level and also discusses briefly the forces and individuals involved in making the decisions that go into the final budget.

The budget process in the United States has undergone numerous changes through the history of the republic. For the first 132 years, Congress controlled the finances of the federal government, with minor exceptions. With the increasing involvement of the federal government in the economy and changes in the economic system, congressional control began to erode while that of the executive increased. In the 1921 Budget and Accounting Act Congress reorganized the budgetary function of the executive branch. The trend toward executive branch dominance in the budgetary process was arrested with the passage of the Congressional Budget and Impoundment Control Act of 1974, which restored to Congress some of the power over budget making it had lost and provided it with better means and greater responsibility for controlling the budget.

Decisions on the federal budget are made during the course of a lengthy and complex process. The final outcome is determined by the interplay of the executive and the Congress, with all individuals and groups involved trying to act (for the most part) in accordance with their own version of the public interest. The budget-making process is such that no one individual or agency dominates the choice of taxes and expenditures, or the size of the federal debt.

Although Congress ultimately bears the responsibility for budget decisions, the executive branch of the government is charged with the preparation and submission of the budget. Until 1976, the President in his budget message to Congress in January would submit his budget for the fiscal year which began July 1 and ended June 30. The Congressional Budget and Impoundment Control Act of 1974 changed the dates of the fiscal year: beginning in 1976, the fiscal year runs from October 1 through September 30, with a transition quarter running from July 1 to September 30, 1976. Aside from changing the fiscal year, the 1974 act did not directly alter the executive budget process (except in regard to certain submissions and the budget timetable) nor eliminate any existing procedure for the authorization of programs or the appropriation of funds; the new budget process was added to these. The major impact of this act is on the legislative side of budget making and thus is expected to generate some changes in congressional-executive fiscal relations.

Although budgeting is a continuing process, the term "budget cycle" is often used to emphasize its periodicity. There are clearly defined phases of budgeting in most budgetary systems. At the federal level in the United States, four phases can be identified: (1) executive preparation and submission, (2) congressional action, (3) execution and control, and (4) review and audit.

Executive Preparation and Submission

The Congressional Budget and Impoundment Control Act of 1974 requires the executive branch of the federal government beginning in 1975 to submit to Congress a "current services budget" by November 10 for the new fiscal year that starts the following October 1. On the basis of the programs and funding levels in effect for the ongoing fiscal year (say 1977), the current services budget would detail the costs (for 1978) of continuing the authorized fiscal (1977) programs without policy change. The administration is required to spell out its economic assumptions (inflation, unemployment, real rate of economic growth) as part of the current services report. Thus, the current services budget would project spending requirements under *existing* legislation and be based on assumptions of the administration about economic conditions and about programs that are routinely renewed (for example, revenue sharing or earned income tax credit), but before any program expansions, contractions, or new initiatives.[1]

As under past law, the President continues to submit his new budget to Congress in late January or early February (technically, fifteen days after the beginning of each session of the Congress). In addition to the traditional budget details and functional breakdown, the budget document is to include a list of existing tax expenditures (discussed in chapter 2), estimates of expenditures for programs for which funds are appropriated one year in advance, and five-year budget projections of all federal spending under existing programs.

Although the President's budget is scheduled for submission in late January, preparation of the budget begins long before. The budget represents the culmination of about a year of planning and discussion between government agencies and the Office of Management and Budget. The appropriate time sequence of, and the participants in, each stage of budget preparation by the executive branch may be inferred from figure 3-1. The timing suggested is only approximate since it may vary under different pressures or in different departments. Nevertheless, the chart does indicate the lead time required to prepare the executive's budget.

Figure 3-1 illustrates a basic characteristic of budgeting in the executive branch—the two-way flow of decisions up from the agencies and then back down from the OMB and the President.[2] Budget policy development begins at the agency level. By March, or earlier in some cases, the individual organizational units in the departments and agencies make plans for their programs and expenditures. They review current operations, program objectives, issues, and future

1. The Joint Economic Committee is to review and assess the current services budget and report to Congress by December 31.

2. The budget of the Department of Defense is handled somewhat differently from the budgets of other agencies. The Office of Management and Budget staff participates with the financial officers of the Department of Defense in a review of the budget requests of the various services but makes its recommendations to the director of the Office of Management and Budget, while the Defense staff makes independent recommendations to the secretary of defense. In general, final Defense budgetary decisions are made later than those of other agencies.

plans in relation to the upcoming budget. Budget offices in each agency provide information, supporting memorandums, and related materials when, in early spring, requirements for the coming year are submitted to the Office of Management and Budget, which discusses program developments, management issues, and resulting budgetary effects with agency heads. Following these discussions, the OMB advises the President about preliminary agency and department plans and goals. All this information, together with projections of the economic outlook and revenue estimates from the Treasury, the OMB, and the Council of Economic Advisers (in late spring), gives the President the basis for tentative overall budget policy decisions on total outlays, receipts, and major program issues. Guidelines reflecting these policy decisions then flow back down through the OMB to the departments and agencies in the form of planning targets to guide the preparation of the formal budget submissions in September. They must then either modify their programs to fit the guidelines or attempt to justify higher amounts to the OMB and possibly even to the President.

The second phase runs from July through December. This time is spent compiling detailed estimates and negotiating between agencies and the OMB on budget allocations and figures, culminating in the submission of formal estimates to the OMB, where they are analyzed and prepared for review by the director. The review process begins around September or October and ends when all budget issues are resolved, around the end of December. Thus, the budget-making process involves: (1) program-issue orientation of most of the budget process through late spring; (2) compilation and submission of agency estimates in the fall; and (3) budget review and presidential decisions in November and December.

Budget Review: The Director's Letter

The budget process beginning in the early spring is referred to as the spring planning review. The first step in this part of the budget process leads to the submission of a letter from the director of the OMB. In this period of formulating outlays and program issues and developing requests for new programs, the various governmental agencies compete with one another for the federal dollar. During the early spring, the OMB confers with departments and agencies on the coming budget. An important aspect of this early consultation is to

Figure 3-1. Formulation of the President's Budget

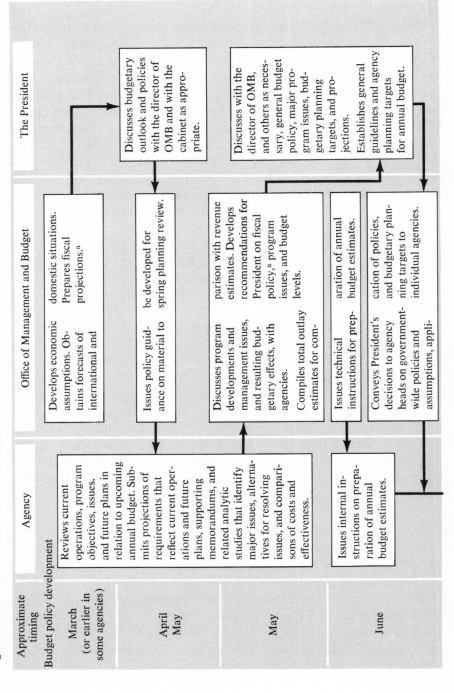

Approximate timing	Agency	Office of Management and Budget	The President
Budget policy development			
March (or earlier in some agencies)		Develops economic assumptions. Obtains forecasts of international and domestic situations. Prepares fiscal projections.[a]	
April May	Reviews current operations, program objectives, issues, and future plans in relation to upcoming annual budget. Submits projections of requirements that reflect current operations and future plans, supporting memorandums, and related analytic studies that identify major issues, alternatives for resolving issues, and comparisons of costs and effectiveness.	Issues policy guidance on material to be developed for spring planning review.	Discusses budgetary outlook and policies with the director of OMB and with the cabinet as appropriate.
May		Discusses program developments and management issues, and resulting budgetary effects, with agencies. Compiles total outlay estimates for comparison with revenue estimates. Develops recommendations for President on fiscal policy,[a] program issues, and budget levels.	Discusses with the director of OMB, and others as necessary, general budget policy, major program issues, budgetary planning targets, and projections. Establishes general guidelines and agency planning targets for annual budget.
June	Issues internal instructions on preparation of annual budget estimates.	Issues technical instructions for preparation of annual budget estimates. Conveys President's decisions to agency heads on government-wide policies and assumptions, application of policies, and budgetary planning targets to individual agencies.	

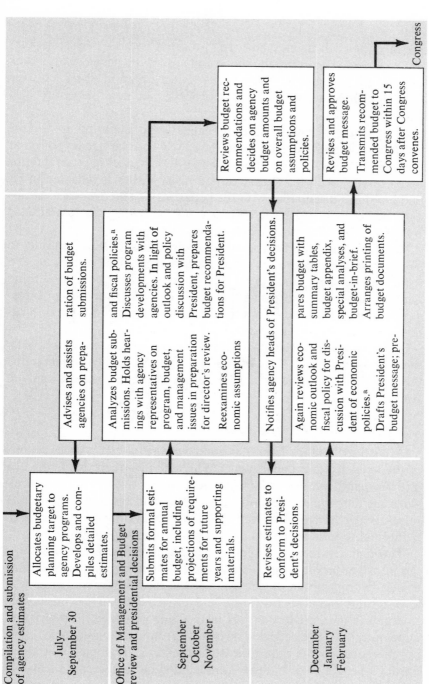

Source: Office of Management and Budget.
a. In cooperation with the Treasury Department and the Council of Economic Advisers.

identify for each agency a set of "program issues"—decisions that must be made regarding the scope and size of the agency's programs and program elements. These partly reflect program issues left over from the previous year's budget process, but new issues are also raised.

The program issues for each agency and department are the product of negotiations between the OMB and the agency, often at the highest levels. The director of the OMB discusses in general terms budget policy with the President and his staff; this is reflected in his and his staff's discussions with the departments and agencies. At this early stage, then, the basic objectives of the budget process already reflect, in a broad sense, the presidential perspective.

The discussions and decisions on program issues lead naturally to simultaneous consideration of the special analytical studies needed from each agency. Since these studies often cannot be geared to an annual budget cycle, plans will be laid for studies over two- or three-year periods, as well as for interim studies to provide limited information for decisionmaking in the current year.

By early summer, the OMB director sends a letter to each department or agency head. This letter formalizes the budget targets set by the President, agreements reached on program issues, and analytic studies for each agency.

Agency Budget Preview Activities

After the director's letter has gone out, the budget process centers in the agencies and departments. The activities there focus on (1) initiation and completion of analytical studies needed to reach decisions on the program issues identified in the director's letter; (2) intra-agency budget reviews; and (3) preparation of budget estimates and reports on analytic studies for submission to the OMB.

Through the agency budgeting office and professional staffs flows the information on programs and costs needed by the administrator to decide on program objectives raised in the director's letter as well as programs and costs for future budget years. Often it is impossible to conduct the needed analysis in the time provided, and program issues may have to be decided on diverse grounds, ranging from political pressures to the administrator's intuitive judgment. Not every agency's programs or budgets are included in the director's letter. A large segment of budget outlays is virtually outside the budget process and is often not reflected in program objectives or issues. For the last few years, for example, such open-ended or fixed cost items as interest on the public debt, social security and other retirement programs, and veterans' pensions have accounted for about 65 percent of total nondefense budget expenses and for about 50 percent of total budget outlays. The levels of these outlays are determined by provisions written into legislation authorizing the programs and by other factors not readily subject to annual budgetary control. They are, however, subject to review, and legislation is frequently proposed to change them. The crucial budget decisions, then, relate primarily to proposed changes in the open-ended programs and to programs subject to budgetary control. They take the form of an evaluation of relatively small increases in costs and activities.

The focus of the budget preview process on program issues and analytical studies should not obscure the fact that budget making is and always will be a *political* process, and at the agency level the politics of budget making are important in several ways. Agencies and their "line people" are expected to be advocates of increased appropriations. It is generally accepted as natural and inevitable by Congress and the OMB that agency budget offices will have a strong interest in justifying their program decisions and appropriation requests. As advocates, the agencies supply information crucial to congressional and OMB decisions—information Congress and the OMB otherwise would have to obtain for themselves.[3]

On the other hand, agencies or departments rarely ask for all the funds they believe they could use. If they did, the OMB or Congress would probably make substantial cuts; to have proposals cut sharply every year would set what the agencies would consider an unfortunate precedent, though some cuts are inevitable in an agency's budget. As guardians of the public purse, the OMB and Congress are expected to be more economy-minded than agency heads, who are responsible for the execution rather than the financing of specific programs. Moreover, the OMB has the task of weighing budget requests across the whole range of federal activity and must make recommendations to the President concerning the choices open to him.

So in making decisions on programs and expenditures, agencies

---

3. For discussion of motivations, aims, and politics of individual agencies, see Aaron Wildavsky, *The Politics of the Budgetary Process* (2d ed., Little, Brown, 1974), chap. 2.

cannot, for strategic reasons, aim too high or too low. Their decision-making will reflect clues and hints from the executive branch, Congress, clientele groups, and their own organizations. In this way they are able in most cases to get a rough idea of what will prove acceptable to the OMB, the President and his advisers, and congressional committees on the budget.

Thus, in the late spring and in the summer, the agencies and departments prepare for the submission of their budget proposals to the OMB. Before the submission date, the agency or department usually has its own preview when internal drafts of analytical studies are submitted, criticized, and revised. Once the department or agency head is satisfied, analytical studies and budget requests are submitted to the OMB, usually in September. Then begins the formal budget review process within the OMB, which will be described later in this chapter.

The Fiscal Side of Budgeting

While the agencies' budget-making process is taking place, the President and his economic advisers are engaged in a continuing parallel process. The President and his advisers review data on economic conditions and future outlook and begin to formulate the fiscal-policy stance they will take for the upcoming fiscal year. Beginning with President Kennedy's term of office and continuing through the Ford administration, the agencies concerned with the overall budget and its impact on the economy—the OMB, the Treasury, and the Council of Economic Advisers—submitted periodic memorandums to the President on current and projected economic conditions. This informal group of agencies, known as the "troika," has in the past had an important influence on budget and fiscal decisionmaking. At present, the Economic Policy Group, which supersedes the troika at the highest level, performs such a function. The President has periodic discussions with the Economic Policy Group, sometimes joined by the chairman of the Federal Reserve Board, and receives frequent memorandums from them. In the spring, the President receives projections of the economic outlook prepared jointly by the Council of Economic Advisers, the Treasury, and the OMB, and reviewed by the Economic Policy Group. The President also receives projections of estimated receipts from the Treasury Department. Out of the various discussions and memorandums comes the President's decision on tax and expenditure policy.

At the end of the spring planning review, the director of the OMB and his staff deal directly with the President and his advisers on emerging problems, initial clearance on major program decisions, and the overall revenue and expenditure outlook. By late summer the administration's general budget policy for the forthcoming fiscal year begins to take shape.

Also at the end of the spring planning review, at the time the policy letter based on guidelines received from the President is sent by the director of the OMB to agency and department heads, the general budget policy is translated into budget planning figures of some twenty agencies. These are not ceiling figures; rather, the OMB is informing the agency that, in view of the administration's program, the agency's budget will probably be somewhere near a certain figure. Agencies can bring in estimates exceeding the planning figure, but if they do, they must indicate where they could make cuts if required to adhere to the planning figure. It is at this point that the program and fiscal aspects of the budget process come together.

The Review Process

Throughout the fall and early winter, the executive branch is engaged in a crucial stage in the budget-making process. The agencies and departments conduct intensive examinations of their programs in light of the planning figures or budget directives that have been passed down to them and the previous year's action by Congress. The agency or department that is well within its planning figure seldom has problems (though this situation is so rare as to be completely outside the experience of most career agency budget officers). Most, however, face a difficult decision about where to cut (in the absence of specific directives), or whether to cut at all, or whether to fight it out by appealing to the OMB and, if necessary, to the President.

After the review within the department, estimates are submitted to the OMB and then referred to the budget examiners. The knowledge the examiners possess about the agency, based on long-run experience, field investigation, and the like, is now brought to bear on the estimates. The examiners give considerable attention to the basis for the individual estimate, review the agency's past performance, check the accuracy of the factual information presented, and consider the future implications of the program. Furthermore, the examiners identify programs, budget, and management issues of importance to be raised for discussion with agency representatives during the hearings conducted at the OMB. At these hearings, usually held in October and November, the department or agency presents and defends its programs and budget before the examiner and other OMB staff members.

Relations between agencies and the OMB are important at this stage, particularly the relation between each agency and the OMB examiners assigned to it. On the one hand, the agency is reluctant to incur OMB disfavor, for the OMB's recommendations to the President do carry weight.[4] At the same time, the OMB cannot restrain the agencies too much, for "end runs" by agencies to Congress to get funds disapproved by the OMB are not unusual. So both parties are constrained, and the end result is usually somewhere between what each would prefer.

On the basis of the hearings and his knowledge of agency programs, operations, and overall policies, the OMB examiner, after consultation with the associate director, to whom he reports, submits his recommendations to the director for the "director's review." This is conducted by top staff members of the OMB—the director, the deputy director, and other officials, with the director usually serving as chairman.

Concurrent with the director's review is the last stage of executive budget preparation—presidential review of the budget as it emerges from the OMB and preparation of the annual budget document. After the President's review, his program decisions and approved allowances are sent to each agency head, who may then accept them or appeal them to the OMB or to the President. Another hearing on some of the issues is thus sometimes obtained. At this hectic time, final conclusions are drawn on the economic outlook and prospective revenues, and these, together with the emerging outlay estimates of the OMB, make it possible for the OMB, the Council of Economic Advisers, and the Treasury to recommend last-minute changes that will affect the size of the budget surplus or deficit. These changes may also stimulate final appeals from the departments and agencies.

During the third week in January—somewhat miraculously, considering the coordination and effort involved—the budget document and message are transmitted to Congress.

4. It is important to note that the OMB is an "arm of the President," and is not itself a formulator of policy except insofar as the director influences presidential decisions. That is, it is a staff agency.

Congressional Authorization

Until 1975, Congress took action on the President's budget in a piecemeal fashion. Spending proposals were acted upon one at a time and tax measures were treated separately. This process offered Congress no opportunity to look at both sides of the budget as a unified proposal, to consider whether the resulting budget deficit or surplus was consistent with the needs of the economy, or whether the budget priorities implied in individual spending and tax measures reflected overall national priorities.

With the passage of the Congressional Budget and Impoundment Control Act of 1974, Congress acquired a new budget process. The act gave Congress a mechanism for looking at the budget as a whole early in the budget cycle and explicitly addressing questions of fiscal policy. The existing tax and appropriations committees have retained their functions, but their decisions, under the new act, must be consistent with the overall budget totals fixed by Congress on the recommendations of the newly created budget committees.

Congressional review begins when the President transmits his current services estimates to Congress in November, some two months before the President's budget is submitted. Although the current services estimates do not reflect the President's recommendations or the actual budget figures to be submitted later, they serve as a basis upon which Congress can proceed to examine the President's budget to be submitted in January. Congress can act as it wishes on the President's budget proposals—changing programs, increasing or decreasing requests, acting upon legislation determining taxes, and determining the levels of the national debt.

Terminology

Before discussing the congressional budget process, the terms used in that process will be defined: budget authority, obligations, appropriations, continuing resolution, and outlays.

The budget document, *The Budget of the United States Government,* issued in January of each year, sets forth the President's proposals for the federal government's outlays and budget authority for the ensuing fiscal year. Congress does not vote on outlays directly, but rather on *budget authority;* that is, Congress first enacts legislation that authorizes an agency to carry out a particular program such as food stamps or revenue sharing, but does not provide funds for it. This enactment is called *authorization*. Many programs are authorized for a specific number of years, while others, such as space, defense procurement, or foreign affairs, require annual authorization.[5] The granting of budget authority is usually a separate subsequent action.

Budget authority permits *obligations* to be incurred by government agencies. Such obligations include liabilities for salaries, interest, supplies, construction, and the like. For most accounts the amount of the authority is related to the obligations that it is expected will be incurred during this year. Budget authority usually takes the form of *appropriations,* which permit obligations to be incurred and payments made. Some budget authority takes the form of *contract authority,* which permits agencies to incur obligations before appropriations but requires a subsequent appropriation to liquidate (that is, to pay) these obligations. There is also *borrowing authority,* which authorizes agencies to use borrowed money to incur obligations and to make payments. Where such authority applies to the use of Treasury borrowing, it is called *authority to spend federal debt receipts,* and where it applies to agency borrowing either directly from the public or from government-administered funds, it is called *authority to spend agency debt receipts.*

Since appropriations are not usually considered until authorizing legislation is passed, many agencies in recent years have received their appropriations late in the congressional session after the new fiscal year has begun. When an agency does not receive its new appropriation before the old one lapses, it operates under a *continuing resolution* passed by Congress. This continuing resolution allows the agency to spend at the previous year's rate. Appropriations come in several forms, ranging from one-year appropriations, which allow an agency to incur obligations only during one fiscal year (the most common form), to no-year appropriations, which are available until the purpose of the spending is accomplished.[6] Generally, if the obli-

5. Authorizing legislation for a new activity lasting more than one fiscal year is submitted for at least two fiscal years of the program.

6. Most trust fund appropriations are permanent, as are many federal fund appropriations, such as the appropriation to pay interest on the public debt.

gational authority is not used during the specified period, it lapses and is no longer available to the agency unless Congress specifically passes the appropriation again. Appropriations for reappropriations of this sort are counted as budget authority in the year of the congressional action.

Obligations are liquidated by the issuance of checks. Payments made are called *outlays*. Outlays out of new budget authority must be obligated within a certain period but need not actually be paid within that period. Even in the case of one-year appropriations, the agency is not required to pay the bills that year (for example, payment need not be made until after deliveries have been made).

Since budget authority may be granted for a period longer than the fiscal year, there is always a substantial carry-over of unobligated authority (called *unobligated balances*) from previous years. There is also a carry-over of unspent obligations (called *obligated balances*) from the previous year or two—that is, a carry-over of budget authority that has been committed but not spent. Thus the outlay totals in a budget reflect outlays expected to be made during the coming fiscal year out of uncommitted budget authority, as well as obligated balances carried over from previous years and out of new budget authority requested in the current budget.

As figure 3-2 shows, the 1977 budget requested $433.4 billion of new authority, which, with unspent budget authority of $519.6 billion carried over from prior years and transferred from off-budget agencies, made a total of $953 billion available to the agencies. Of this, $394.2 billion was expected to be spent during fiscal year 1977. Some $112.9 billion derived from unspent authority carried over and $281.3 billion from new authority. With budget authority for $4.0 billion expiring, about $554.8 billion of unspent authority would remain for years after fiscal 1977.

Once budget authority is granted, the Congressional Budget and Impoundment Control Act of 1974 requires that any amount not spent be reported to Congress in rescission or deferral messages for congressional action.[7] Impoundments take effect unless they are disapproved by both houses of Congress within forty-five days of the President's notification; deferrals are effective until overturned by either house.

7. A deferral means the temporary withholding of funds from obligation.

Figure 3-2. Relation of Budget Authority to Outlays, Proposed Federal Budget, Fiscal Year 1977
Billions of dollars

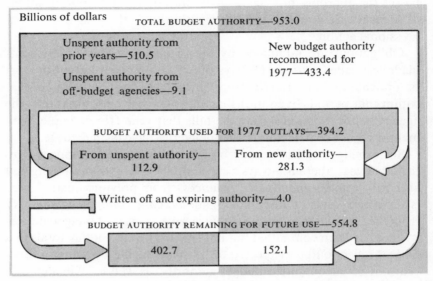

Congressional Budgeting

The congressional side of budgeting was strengthened by the passage of the 1974 act, under which Congress is to consider budget totals before completing action on individual appropriations. The act introduced the following changes:

1. It set up a budget committee in each house, which, using reports from the Congressional Budget Office also established by the act and from the various committees of the Congress, studies budget options and prepares budget resolutions.

2. It required Congress, before action on appropriations or spending measures, to adopt concurrent *budget resolutions,* first setting target figures for new budget authority and budget outlays as well as the appropriate levels of federal receipts, the budget surplus or deficit, and the public debt and later setting ceilings and floors on these totals.

3. It changed the fiscal year to October 1–September 30 and provided a firm budget schedule for Congress.

4. It changed the rules on impoundment of funds by the President.

The purpose of the new budget committees is to give Congress a better perspective on budget totals and fiscal policy requirements. The House Budget Committee has twenty-five members: five each from the House Appropriations and Ways and Means Committees, thirteen from other standing committees, and one each from the majority and minority leadership. The Senate Budget Committee has sixteen members whose selection has been made by the Democratic and Republican Conferences in accordance with normal selection processes.[8]

The new committees have been given general jurisdiction over the congressional budget process and related matters. Specifically, they are required to report two concurrent resolutions on the budget each year, to study the effects of existing and proposed legislation on federal spending, and to oversee operations of the new Congressional Budget Office.

The CBO—congressional counterpart of the Office of Management and Budget—is a nonpartisan informational and analytical arm of Congress with broad authority to obtain data from executive agencies. The CBO is headed by a director, appointed to a four-year term by the Speaker of the House and the president pro tempore of the Senate. The act specifies the CBO's duties according to priorities: (1) to furnish the House and Senate Budget Committees with information relating to all matters within their jurisdiction; (2) to supply the House Ways and Means Committee, the Senate Finance Committee, and the appropriations committees with all available data related to the budget and to make budget-related studies at their request; (3) to give other congressional committees available information and undertake studies on their behalf; and (4) to supply all members of Congress with relevant available information.

The CBO is also required by the act to submit an annual report to the House and Senate Budget Committees setting forth budget alternatives and national budget priorities as well as tax expenditures. This report must be submitted by April 1. Moreover the office must issue periodic scorekeeping reports, five-year budget projections, and cost analyses of legislation reported by all committees other than the appropriations committees.

8. Under the conference agreement, Senate Budget Committee meetings are open to the public unless the committee votes for a secret review in circumstances spelled out in the act.

Budget Submission

In moving the government to an October 1–September 30 fiscal year, the act expanded the congressional "budget season" to nine months, giving Congress a longer period to shape the budget than in the past. The congressional budget process begins around November 10 of each year, with the submission of a current services budget. The Joint Economic Committee reviews the current services budget and reports its evaluation to Congress by December 31. As under prior law, the President submits his revised federal budget to Congress about January 20.

First Budget Resolution

After receiving the President's budget proposals and after considering advice from the CBO and other committees, the House and Senate Budget Committees draw up, reconcile, and report a first concurrent resolution to their respective houses by April 15 of each year.[9] Floor consideration of the budget resolution takes place under special rules devised to expedite the proceedings so that adoption of the first concurrent resolution does not take place after May 15.[10] May 15 is also the date by which legislative committees must report authorizing legislation for the ensuing fiscal year.[11]

The first concurrent resolution is a tentative budget. It sets target totals for budget authority, outlays, receipts, and the public debt to guide Congress in its subsequent consideration of appropriations and tax measures. The resolution also includes any recommendation for changes in tax revenues or in the level of the debt ceiling.

Within these overall targets, the resolution breaks down budget authority and outlays into seventeen major functions (defense, health, and so on). The functional targets are intended to represent broad

9. The CBO issues budget scorekeeping reports on the status of congressional action on the budget. These reports represent a way of measuring congressional budget action against the budget targets established by Congress in the first concurrent resolution.

10. Because this and subsequent budget determinations are in the form of concurrent resolutions they will not have the force of law nor will they directly limit actual outlays.

11. There would be two exemptions from the May 15 deadline for reporting authorization legislation: those dealing with social security programs and entitlement legislation that cannot be considered on the floor until the budget resolution has been cleared.

priorities and not to make judgments on the specific goals within each function. The latter is subsequently determined by congressional committees.

Congressional Consideration of Spending and Tax Measures

The congressional budget timetable and budget process are shown in table 3-1 and figure 3-3. Congressional action on requests for appropriations and for changes in revenue laws continues to follow the old pattern: appropriations are considered within the appropriations

Table 3-1. Congressional Budget Timetable

Deadline date	Action to be completed
November 10	Current services budget submitted
15 days after Congress meets	President's budget submitted
March 15	Reports of congressional committees submitted to budget committees
April 1	Report of Congressional Budget Office submitted to budget committees
April 15	Budget committees report first concurrent resolution on the budget to House and Senate
May 15	Committees report bills authorizing new budget authority
May 15	First concurrent resolution on the budget passed by Congress
7th day after Labor Day	All appropriation bills passed by Congress
September 15	Final action on second concurrent resolution on the budget completed by Congress
September 25	Final action on reconciliation for second concurrent resolution completed by Congress
October 1	Fiscal year begins

committees and subcommittees, while revenue measures are taken up by the Ways and Means Committee. The process is the same as in the past, but subject to the guidelines of the first concurrent resolution on the budget. The budget resolution *guides* but does not *bind* Congress in acting on appropriations and revenue bills.

After enactment of the first concurrent resolution, Congress begins processing appropriations requests for the upcoming fiscal year according to an established pattern.[12] These requests are considered first

12. Not all budget authority is approved through the appropriation process. That which is not is called backdoor spending.

Figure 3-3. The Congressional Budget Process

Month	Action	Ongoing
June		CBO issues periodic scorekeeping reports comparing congressional action with first concurrent resolution [sec. 308(b)]
July	To extent practicable, CBO cost analyses and five-year projections will accompany all reported public bills, except appropriation bills [sec. 403] Reports on new budget authority and tax expenditure bills must contain comparisons with first concurrent resolution and five-year projections [sec. 308(a)] If a committee reports new entitlement legislation that exceeds appropriate allocation in latest concurrent resolution, it shall be referred to the appropriations committee with instructions to report its recommendations within 15 days [sec. 401(b)(2)]	
August	Budget committees prepare second concurrent resolution and report	
September	Seventh day after Labor Day: Congress completes action on all budget and spending authority bills [sec. 309] 15: Congress completes action on second concurrent resolution [sec. 301(a), (b)] *Thereafter, neither house may consider any bill, amendment, or conference report that would result in an increase over budget outlay or authority figures or a reduction in revenue level adopted in second concurrent resolution* [sec. 311(a)] 25: Congress completes action on reconciliation bill or resolution [sec. 310(c)–(e)] *Congress may not adjourn until it completes action on second concurrent resolution—and reconciliation, if any* [sec. 310(f)]	
October	Fiscal year begins	

Congressional action on spending bills

Adoption of second concurrent resolution and reconciliation

October	1: Fiscal year begins [sec. 501]	
November	10: President submits current services budget [sec. 605(a)]	CBO five-year projections (as soon as possible after October 1) [sec. 308(c)]
December	31: Joint Economic Committee reports analysis of current services budget to budget committees [sec. 605(b)]	
January	Approximately last week of month: President submits budget (15 days after Congress convenes) [sec. 601]	
February		
March	15: All committees and joint committees submit estimates and views to budget committees [sec. 301(c)] — Legislation providing contract or borrowing authority must be made subject to amounts provided in appropriation acts [sec. 401(a)]	Budget committees hold hearings; begin work on first concurrent resolution [sec. 301(d)]
April	1: CBO report to budget committees [sec. 202(f)] — 1–15: Budget committees report first concurrent resolution (on or before April 15) [sec. 301(d)]	House and Senate consider first concurrent resolution [sec. 305] — Conference action and adoption of conference report [sec. 305] — Conference report accompanied by joint explanatory statement, which allocates total levels of budget authority and outlays among committees [sec. 302(b)]
May	Congress—until seventh day after Labor Day—enacts appropriations and spending bills — 15: Congress completes action on first concurrent resolution [sec. 301(a)] — 15: Deadline for committees to report authorization bills (some exceptions, and waiver procedure) [sec. 402(a)–(e)]	Before adoption of concurrent resolution, neither house may consider new budget authority or spending authority bills, revenue changes, or debt limit changes (some exceptions, and waiver procedure) [sec. 303(a)–(c)] — Before reporting first regular appropriation bill, House Appropriations Committee, to extent practicable, marks up all regular appropriation bills and submits to House summary report comparing proposed outlays and budget authority levels with first concurrent resolution [sec. 307] — After adoption of first concurrent resolution, each committee subdivides its allocation among its subcommittees, and promptly reports such subdivisions to its house [sec. 302(b)]

Information gathering, analysis, and preparation of first concurrent resolution

Adoption of first concurrent resolution

Source: House Budget Committee. Section numbers are from the Congressional Budget and Impoundment Control Act of 1974.

in the House of Representatives. The House Appropriations Committee, through its thirteen subcommittees, studies appropriations requests and examines each agency's performance in detail. Each subcommittee is responsible for reporting out one or occasionally two appropriations bills, of which there are thirteen or fourteen in each congressional session. Hearings are held and testimony is given by the relevant agency and its budget officers. After the hearings, the subcommittee goes into executive session and decides on the recommendations it will make. The recommendations are usually accompanied by reasons for the subcommittee's action and by comments on the agency's programs, efficiency, and personnel.

The subcommittee's recommendations and reports are then sent to the full committee for action. The recommendations go to the House where they are debated with the House sitting as a committee of the whole.

Following action by the House, the appropriations and tax bills are forwarded to the Senate, where a similar process is followed. The initial work on appropriations proposals is done in the subcommittees (of which there are thirteen) of the Appropriations Committee. As in the House, they hold hearings, make agreed-upon changes in the bill, and send it to the full committee.

On the floor of the Senate, discussion of appropriations and tax measures is more extensive than it is in the House as a result of the Senate's privilege of unlimited debate. Senate-House differences on appropriations (and on tax bills) are reconciled by a conference committee consisting of members of both houses. The Conference Committee report is returned to the House and Senate for further consideration. If agreed to by both houses, the legislation is transmitted to the President for his approval or veto.

Before the congressional budget act of 1974, it was customary to report any appropriations bill out to the floor when it had been approved by the full committee. The new act, however, directs the House Appropriations Committee to try to complete action on all its appropriations and to submit a summary report before reporting the first bill for floor action.

Also, under the new act all appropriations bills must be passed by the seventh day after Labor Day. However, the deadline will not apply if consideration of appropriations is delayed because necessary authorization legislation has not been enacted in time. In this case, appropriations bills may be held up until after the final action on the conference report or until reconciliation.

Second Budget Resolution and Reconciliation Process

After finishing action on all bills by September 15, Congress is required to take another overall look at budget totals. A second concurrent resolution is passed, either affirming or revising the budget targets set by the initial resolution. The resolution adopted will contain budget ceilings, by function, for budget authority and outlays. It also sets a floor for revenue measures. If separate congressional decisions taken during the appropriations process are not consistent with the second concurrent budget resolution totals, the resolution may direct that changes be made in budget authority (new or carried over from previous years), entitlements, receipts, or the public debt. This resolution also instructs the committee with jurisdiction over the prescribed changes to report implementing legislation. The House and Senate Budget Committees then combine these changes and report them to the floor in the form of a reconciliation bill. By September 25, Congress completes the reconciliation process, thereby enacting the second concurrent resolution. Congress cannot adjourn for the year until the reconciliation legislation is passed.

With the enactment of the reconciliation bill, the congressional budget process is completed. At this point Congress may not consider any spending or revenue legislation that would make budget figures differ from those specified in the second resolution. However, Congress may, if the need arises, adopt a new budget resolution during the fiscal year.

If action on appropriations is not completed by the beginning of the fiscal year, Congress may enact a *continuing resolution* to provide the agencies affected with authority to continue operating at previous year levels until their regular appropriations are enacted.

Budget Execution and Control

Once the budget is approved by Congress, it becomes the financial basis for the operations of government agencies during the fiscal year. How is budget authority granted by Congress to an agency or department converted into outlays?

Apportionment and Allotment

When the appropriations bill is enacted, an appropriations warrant, drawn by the Treasury and countersigned by the General Accounting Office, is sent to the agency. The agency reviews and revises its budget in light of the appropriations bill and, within ten days of the appropriations bill's passage, submits to the Office of Management and Budget a request for apportionment. Apportionment may be defined as the rate at which budget authority can be used, and the authority is usually apportioned by quarters over the period of the appropriation, both to ensure that the budget authority is not spent faster than Congress intended and to ensure the most economical and effective use of the funds.

The OMB approves or revises the agency apportionment request; in effect, the OMB is the apportioning authority. The power of apportionment gives the executive some latitude in controlling the direction and timing of federal outlays. Within the individual agencies, the use of budget authority apportioned by the OMB is controlled through a similar device. The breakdown of apportionment by organizational unit is called *allotment*.

Obligations Incurred and Outlays

With few exceptions, the various agencies actually incur obligations only after apportionment by the OMB. The incurring of obligations, however, does not necessarily mean immediate cash expenditures. In some cases, the expenditure of funds virtually coincides with the incurring of obligations; in others, the actual expenditure of funds may lag considerably behind.

In two kinds of commitment, the time lag between obligations and outlays is very short. Outlays for the purchase of existing assets (except land, where the lag may be considerable) and for payments such as social security benefits, veterans' pensions, and unemployment compensation, coincide with—or are very close to—the incurring of the obligations. Government expenditures for services (in particular, those of government employees) also typically occur close to the time of commitment.

But when the federal government contracts with the private sector to employ resources on its behalf—that is, when the federal government buys goods and services produced by the private sector—the lag of outlays behind obligations may be substantial. This lag is both administrative and operational; it takes private producers time to draw plans, negotiate with subcontractors, and deliver the product. Some of the economic impact on the private sector (as discussed in chapter 6) thus occurs long before actual delivery of goods and payment, since the producers must employ resources in order to produce goods.

Outlays

When they occur, outlays are generally made from Treasury deposits at the twelve Federal Reserve Banks, which are part of the "Account of the Treasurer of the United States." This account consists mostly of the Treasury checking accounts at the Federal Reserve Banks and at commercial banks. Federal disbursing officers make payment by issuing checks against the Federal Reserve Bank accounts on the basis of vouchers approved by certifying officers of the various agencies; the amount that can be issued is set by the agency's budget authority and the apportionment of it by the OMB. The checks are usually deposited in commercial banks, which then receive a credit to their Federal Reserve Bank accounts. The Federal Reserve Bank charges the Treasury account with the amount of the check and sends the check to the Treasury, where the checks that have been cashed are verified against the record of checks that have been issued.

It is the Treasury's responsibility to maintain adequate working balances in the Federal Reserve Banks to meet payments as they are made. For this purpose, amounts are funneled by the Treasury into Federal Reserve accounts from deposits at commercial banks made directly by district officers of the Internal Revenue Service and from receipts from debt issues.

During the fiscal year, changes in laws or economic conditions may necessitate the enactment of additional budget authority. In this case, supplemental requests are sent to Congress for its consideration. On the other hand, the President may wish, for policy reasons, to withhold some of the appropriated funds. In this case, the President must send a special message to Congress requesting a "rescission" or a "deferral" as required by the new act. Budget authority proposed for rescission must be made available for obligations unless both the House and Senate pass a bill authorizing rescission within forty-five

days of contiguous session as defined in the act. A deferral message—
a temporary withholding of funds from obligation—would remain
in effect for the fiscal year (though not beyond) unless overturned by
a simple majority in either house.

Audit

The individual agencies and departments are responsible for ensuring that the obligations they incur, and the resulting outlays, are
legal according to authorizing and appropriations legislation. The
Congress, however, may obtain an independent check through the
General Accounting Office, which is headed by the comptroller general. The GAO audits the books of the administrative offices responsible for the custody and use of public funds. It also plays an important role in supervising the accounting systems of agencies and
departments and in ensuring that the methods of reporting result in
full disclosure of the receipt and use of funds.

Three major types of audits are made by the GAO. The *comprehensive* audit, the most important, concentrates on the accounting
and reporting system used by a particular agency and checks transactions selectively. The *general* audit examines the accounts of
agency disbursing and certifying officers to determine the legality of
each transaction. If illegal or improper handling of receipts or outlays
is discovered, recovery procedures are instituted by the GAO against
the responsible officer. Finally, the *commercial* audit is applied to
government corporations and enterprises. No recovery is possible in
this case, but Congress is informed of questionable or improper practices.

The annual report and the results of GAO audits are transmitted to
Congress by the comptroller general. The results of special investi-
gations of particular agencies are referred to the House and Senate
Committees on Government Operations.

In addition, the comptroller general is required, under the Congressional Budget and Impoundment Control Act of 1974, to monitor
the executive branch's messages to Congress on proposed rescissions
and deferrals. Should the President fail to comply with congressional
actions that overrule impoundment of funds, the comptroller general
can ask the court to issue an order requiring the release of impounded
funds in accordance with the Congressional Budget and Impoundment Control Act of 1974.

Improvements in the Budget Process

Budget procedures and the budget process reflect a number of improvements made in the last twenty-five years or so in the executive and congressional phases of the budget determination. These are summarized below.

Changes in the Budget Document and Budget Message

A comparison of budget messages of recent years with that of 1972 shows that much greater emphasis is now being placed on the relation of federal finances to conditions in the national economy. Three important dimensions have been emphasized in recent budgets: (1) an element of economic policy; (2) a definition of the boundaries between responsibilities of the private and public sectors; and (3) a reflection of the President's sense of priorities. The 1977 and 1978 federal budget documents clearly state these dimensions and provide comprehensive but concise analysis of federal budget programs using graphs and other illustrations.

A MORE COMPACT BUDGET VOLUME. Beginning with the budget for fiscal year 1963, a major improvement was introduced in the presentation of the budget. Unlike previous budget documents, which were printed on outsize pages and were as thick as a large city telephone directory, that budget was 368 pages of ordinary book size, and included facts and figures most users of the budget normally need, while relegating the details of appropriations proposals and programs used by the congressional committees to an appendix volume. The budget for fiscal year 1978 has grown to 456 pages.

The contents of the budget were affected in several ways by the passage of the Congressional Budget and Impoundment Control Act of 1974. Beginning with fiscal year 1976, the budget document contains estimates of tax expenditures for the budget year, detailed five-year projections of estimated outlays, budget authority, and receipts, estimates for the following fiscal year for any program for which advance appropriations have been authorized, and comparisons of actual outlays and of receipts for the last complete fiscal year with the previously estimated figures for that year.

THE BUDGET IN BRIEF. Beginning in 1950, the Office of Management and Budget (or its predecessor, the Bureau of the Budget) has published each year a pamphlet presenting in popular form some of the more significant data relating to the budget and federal finance. Recently, the budget in brief has been improved and expanded to cover the most important aspects of the federal budget.

SPECIAL ANALYSES. The budget document has also been improved by the addition of several special analyses. The budget transmitted in January 1950 and succeeding budgets have contained an analysis of "investment, operating, and other budget expenditures [later called outlays]," dividing budget outlays into additions to federal assets, expenditures for nonfederal physical assets and other developmental purposes, current expenses for aids and special services, and other current operating expenses. The budget for 1963 presented for the first time an analysis of federal receipts and expenditures on a national income accounts basis. Other special analyses have dealt with federal aid to state and local governments, federal debt, federal credit programs, federal research and development programs, and federal government statistical programs. These analyses are now collected in a separate volume, *Special Analyses,* which accompanies the annual budget volume.

OTHER CHANGES IN THE BUDGET DOCUMENT. Other changes have also markedly improved the budget. The budgets of all agencies were first broken down by program or activity in the budget presented in 1950, which made congressional appraisal easier, and in the same year a narrative statement of the results expected from each expenditure of funds was introduced. Recommendations for new budget authority were first totaled as a separate category in the fiscal year 1952 budget. A comparison of unspent budget authority, new budget authority, and outlays was included beginning with the budget presented in 1954. Obligations incurred were given separate treatment in the budget for fiscal year 1958 but were not summarized in a table by agency until the 1962 budget. Also introduced in the 1962 budget was a recapitulation of employment for the government as a whole.

The Unified Budget Concept

Beginning with fiscal year 1969, a new budget concept was introduced while others were dropped. In the previous years, different budget concepts—administrative, consolidated cash statement, and national income accounts—had been used. The unified budget concept (presented in January 1968) was adopted as the official format, while administrative and cash budgets were abandoned. Since 1969 the unified budget concept has been the only budget concept used in the President's budget.

Improvement in Budget Presentation

In addition to the above improvements, the presentation of the budget to Congress has also been improved through oral testimony by the director of the OMB and the secretary of the treasury before the budget committees, appropriations committees, and the Joint Economic Committee. This procedure enables those committees to gain some understanding of the President's budget priorities before it acts on budget totals as well as on the specific pieces assigned to the various subcommittees.

Improvements in the Congressional Phase of Budgeting

The most signal achievement in the history of congressional budget making is undoubtedly the passage of the Congressional Budget and Impoundment Control Act of 1974. The act established a new and well-laid-out budget process. By requiring both houses of Congress to vote on budget totals before deliberating on appropriation requests, it has eliminated a major weakness of congressional budget practice —the practice of looking at separate appropriation bills on a piece- meal basis. Moreover, by endowing Congress with three new instru- mentalities (two budget committees and the Congressional Budget Office), it has given Congress the access to information and the staff it needs to determine national budget priorities and policies. And finally, by focusing congressional attention on all legislation affecting aggregate spending and taxation for the upcoming fiscal year, it has facilitated congressional appraisal of fiscal policy.

Remaining Problems

However, problems still remain in the budget process. The most crucial is the lack of long-term budget planning. Although the new act requires the executive branch and the Congressional Budget Office to present five-year budget projections, the one-year budget still domi- nates congressional budget-making efforts. Since it focuses most of its attention on the one-year budget, Congress cannot effectively translate domestic and foreign policy issues into budgets. To do so would require Congress to consider budget programs for several years ahead, set goals for future years, and then work back to the current budget.[13]

Another weakness still remaining in the budget process relates to the "uncontrollability" of the budget. In any one year, much of the budget is "locked in" before the congressional review begins because a great deal of spending derives from programs for which expenditures are mandatory, such as interest on the debt and social security. This means that no dramatic change in programs or program elements, size, or budget priorities can take place in any one year even if national priorities demand it. Only marginal budget changes are made. Eliminating the mandatory features of government programs would make the budget process more flexible, but it would work against many other objectives. A more systematic examination of locked-in expenditures, however, might reduce budget uncontrollability.

The Carter administration is attempting to control the budget by introducing the so-called zero-base budgeting technique.[14] As the name implies, this is a method that starts from the position that every agency's base contains no programs and no funding. Every program would then have to be examined, evaluated, and justified in terms of alternatives and the nation's budget priorities. To do this would require examination of specific agencies on a rotating basis once every few years, an enormous outlay of effort on the part of the agencies and the OMB, and the development of analytical techniques for evaluating government programs. Zero-base budgeting is being used for the first time in the preparation of the fiscal 1979 budget.

13. See "Prepared Statement of Hon. Alice M. Rivlin," in *Five-Year Budget Projections,* Hearings before the Subcommittee on Priorities and Economy in Government of the Joint Economic Committee, 94:1 (GPO, 1976), pp. 18–22.

14. For discussions on this technique, see *Zero-Base Budget Legislation,* Hearings before the Task Force on Budget Process of the House Committee on the Budget, 94:2 (GPO, 1976).

CHAPTER FOUR

The Record:
Federal Spending and Taxes

A DISCUSSION of federal budget policy can benefit from the perspective provided by a brief look at the past record of federal spending and taxation. Statistics are available to provide a view of the growth of the federal budget virtually from the birth of the nation.

In addition to the general trends in federal outlays and taxes, the review will include the record of budget deficits and surpluses, with an analysis of the extent to which actual outlays and receipts have differed from budget estimates. The discussion will consider the degree to which the nation's priorities, as they are reflected in the budget, have changed over the entire history of the United States, but especially since World War II. The chapter closes with a consideration of whether government outlays can be controlled.

Trends in Federal Outlays

The growth of the federal government's outlays over roughly the past two centuries (less a decade or so) is impressive. In 1794, for example, the federal government spent about $7 million; in fiscal

Figure 4-1. Federal Outlays, 1794–1976ᵃ

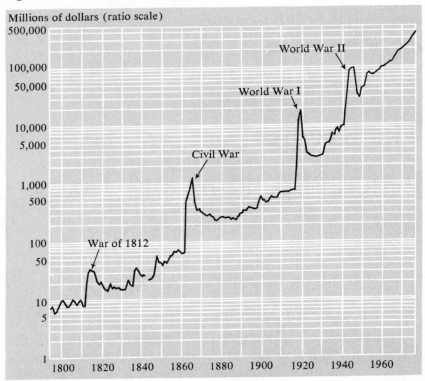

Sources: Data for 1794–1939 from M. Slade Kendrick, *A Century and a Half of Federal Expenditures,* occasional paper 48 (revised) (National Bureau of Economic Research, 1955), pp. 74–78; data for 1940–76 from *The Budget of the United States Government, Fiscal Year 1978,* p. 437.

a. Calendar years through 1842; fiscal years ending June 30 beginning with 1844. The 1843 data cover only the period January through June.

year 1977, federal outlays in the unified budget were estimated at over $400 billion, about 60,000 times those of 1794.

The pattern of this striking growth in federal outlays is shown in figure 4-1.[1] The most obvious influence on the pattern has been war.

1. A technical point: the unified budget was first introduced with the fiscal year 1969 budget. Since that time, budgets for fiscal years 1940–68 have been recast on the same basis. Before fiscal year 1940, however, use must be made of figures based on the consolidated cash budget. The principal difference between this and the unified budget is that the consolidated budget did not net out as many proprietary receipts as does the unified budget. It is unlikely that this (or other relatively minor differences) disturbs the continuity of the series very much. For ten of the fourteen fiscal years 1940–53, for example, the differences between outlays on a consolidated and on a unified basis amount to less, and usually much less, than 3 percent of unified budget outlays.

Large expansions of federal spending occurred during the War of 1812, the Civil War, World War I, and World War II. The trend of federal outlays over the past 183 years may be described as a series of plateaus. Wars have pushed federal spending sharply upward. With the return of peace, expenditures have fallen, but never to prewar levels because the wars left a heritage of interest and veterans' expenses. Between wars, expenditures have shown long periods of relative stability or slow growth; but when another war has come along, expenditures have been forced up, eventually leveling off at a higher plateau.

The growth of federal expenditures can best be placed in perspective by comparison with growth in other economic magnitudes. During the 183-year period, the general price level has approximately quadrupled—or, to put it another way, the value of the dollar is perhaps one-fourth its 1794 value. If allowance is made for changes in the general price level by expressing government expenditures in 1926 prices, the rise in spending is much less formidable, as figure 4-2 shows. Whereas outlays in current prices have grown 60,000 times since 1794, outlays expressed in 1926 prices have expanded about 12,000 times. Another useful way to express outlays is on a per capita basis. If allowance is made for a better than fiftyfold growth in population since 1794, outlays (in 1926 prices) for each person are about 250 times the earlier level. Note, however, that even after these adjustments, the basic pattern of war-induced peaks followed by relatively stable plateaus is still plainly visible.

Perhaps the most significant measure of the growth of federal spending is the ratio of total federal spending to national output, or gross national product. Many types of federal spending can be expected to increase as the nation's economy expands; more highways must be built to transport more output, growing urban areas require new post offices, and so on. Of course, there are other influences on spending, such as the influence of the international situation on defense spending.

Comparing federal expenditures with GNP is one way of measuring the importance of the government in the total economy.[2] Of total federal spending, only the component "purchases of goods and services" indicates the actual amount of resources absorbed by the government. The other components—transfer payments, net interest

2. For alternative measures, see Joseph Scherer, "How Big Is Government?" *Challenge,* vol. 18 (September–October 1975), pp. 60–62.

Figure 4-2. Total and Per Capita Federal Outlays in 1926 Prices, 1794–1976a

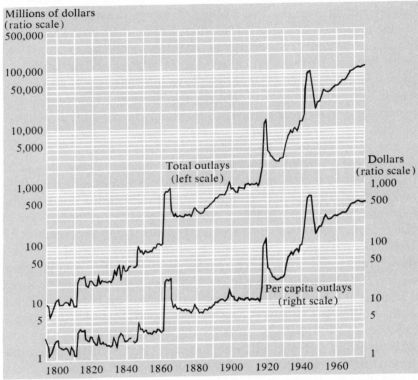

Sources: Expenditures in 1926 prices for 1794–1939 from Kendrick, *A Century and a Half of Federal Expenditures*, pp. 79–83. For 1940–76 they were computed from data used for figure 4-1 and from wholesale price data from *Economic Report of the President, January 1977*, p. 247. (These price statistics are expressed as index numbers with 1967 = 100; they were converted to 1926 = 100 by using series E 23 in U.S. Bureau of the Census, *Historical Statistics of the United States, Colonial Times to 1970*, pt. 1 [GPO, 1975], p. 199.) Per capita outlays in 1926 prices for 1794–1939 from Kendrick, *A Century and a Half of Federal Expenditures*, pp. 84–88. For 1940–76 they were computed by dividing outlays in 1926 prices by population estimates taken from *Historical Statistics*, pt. 1, p. 10, and Bureau of the Census, *Statistical Abstract of the United States, 1976* (GPO, 1976), p. 5.

a. Calendar years through 1842; fiscal years ending June 30 beginning with 1844. The 1843 data cover only the period January through June.

paid, subsidies, and grants-in-aid to state and local governments— represent income channeled through the federal government to the private sector or to the states and their subdivisions which then spend it. However, the sum of these expenditures can usefully be compared with GNP, since they are all part of total federal activity in the economy.

Figure 4-3 shows a rise in federal outlays relative to GNP over the period 1869–1975. From 5 percent in 1869, and a low of 2 percent in 1912–13, the percentage has risen to around 20 percent in recent years. As the data in the figure make clear, most of the rise has taken place since 1930. Except for the World War I years, federal outlays remained about the same relative to GNP from 1869 to 1930. There was a rise during the 1930s and a very sharp rise during World War II; the percentage fell back somewhat after the war but has remained near 20 percent ever since. Purchases of goods and services, an important component of government outlays, have increased at a slower pace because of the growth in importance of transfer payments.

Some light can be shed on the causes of the rise in this percentage since 1930 by classifying federal outlays into "war-connected" and "other" and seeing how these two classes have behaved relative to GNP. War-connected outlays can be defined as military outlays (including military grants to other countries), veterans' outlays, and interest on the federal debt,[3] included because the bulk of currently outstanding debt was issued to finance war. Figure 4-4 presents the relation between war-connected and other outlays and GNP since 1929.

War-connected outlays rose sharply relative to GNP during World War II and the Korean War. In contrast to the rapid demobilization following World War II, however, war-connected outlays following the Korean War remained in the neighborhood of 11–12 percent of GNP through the last half of the 1950s and through the 1960s. In the first half of the 1970s, however, war-connected outlays fell to less than 10 percent of GNP.

Other outlays also rose from 3.8 percent of GNP in fiscal year 1954 to almost 14 percent in fiscal year 1976. Thus the rise in federal outlays can be broken into two fairly distinct periods. From 1929 to the mid-1950s, the rising trend in outlays was primarily the result of rising war-related outlays. Since the mid-1950s, however, other outlays have increased relative to GNP, while war-connected outlays have declined. It is worth examining these trends in somewhat more detail.

3. The classification of outlays into "war-connected" and "other" is found in M. Slade Kendrick, *A Century and a Half of Federal Expenditures*, occasional paper 48 (revised) (National Bureau of Economic Research, 1955).

Figure 4-3. Federal Outlays as a Percentage of Gross National Product, 1869–1975[a]

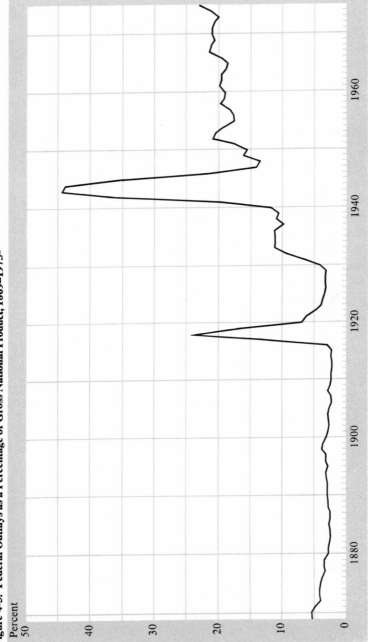

Percent

Sources: Data for 1869–1939 from Kendrick, *A Century and a Half of Federal Expenditures*, pp. 10–12. Data for 1940–75 calculated from *The Budget of the United States Government, Fiscal Year 1978*, p. 437, and *Economic Report of the President, January 1977*, p. 187. Calendar year outlays are approximated by the average level of outlays in the two fiscal years containing the calendar years. For example, outlays in calendar year 1940 are taken to be equal to the average of outlays in fiscal years 1940 and 1941.

a. Calendar years.

Budget Priorities since World War II

Figure 4-4 shows the trend pattern of war-connected and other expenditures relative to GNP during 1929–76. Figure 4-5 presents these outlays by functional category since 1948. Because the purpose of this figure is to provide a more detailed view of the composition of federal outlays, the total of "war-connected" outlays is broken

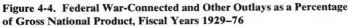

Figure 4-4. Federal War-Connected and Other Outlays as a Percentage of Gross National Product, Fiscal Years 1929–76

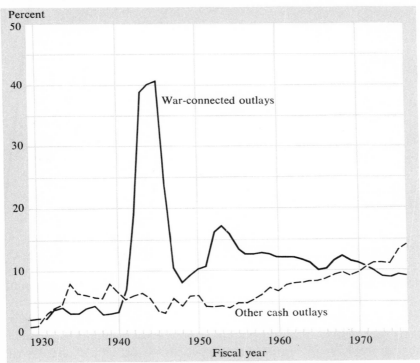

Sources: For 1929–39, other outlays equal total outlays less outlays for the military, veterans, and interest, from Kendrick, *A Century and a Half of Federal Expenditures*, p. 77. For 1940–76, other outlays equal total outlays less outlays for national defense, veterans' benefits and services, and interest, from Office of Management and Budget, Budget Review Division, "Federal Government Finances" (OMB, March 1977; processed). For 1929–46, fiscal year GNP was approximated by the average level of GNP in the two calendar years containing the fiscal year, and for 1947–53, the average in the four quarters; from U.S. Bureau of Economic Analysis, *The National Income and Product Accounts of the United States, 1929–1974: Statistical Tables* (GPO, 1977), table 1.1. GNP figures for fiscal years 1954–76 from *The Budget of the United States Government, Fiscal Year 1978*, p. 435. GNP for 1928 from Bureau of the Census, *Historical Statistics*, pt. 1, p. 228.

Figure 4-5. Outlays by Major Category as a Percentage of Total Outlays, Fiscal Years 1948–76[a]

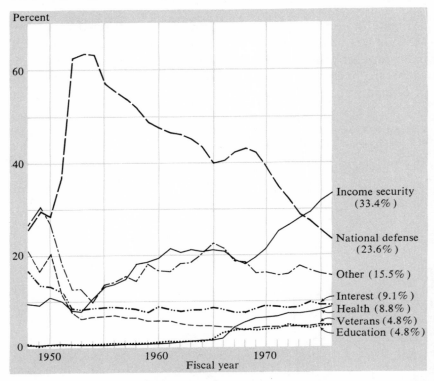

Sources: OMB, "Federal Government Finances" (February 1975; processed), pp. 6–8; *The Budget of the United States Government, Fiscal Year 1978*, pp. 426–31.

a. The numbers in parentheses are the percentages for fiscal year 1976.

down into its components—national defense, veterans' benefits, and interest on the public debt.

As a percentage of the total, outlays on national defense fell in each year of the 1955–65 period; from a level of about 65 percent during the Korean War, they dropped to 40 percent in fiscal year 1965. The Vietnam War saw national defense's share of the budget rise to almost 45 percent, but with the end of the war, this share has resumed its decline. In the fiscal year 1976 budget, national defense accounted for 24 percent of total outlays, its lowest share in the 1948–76 period.

By itself, this decline in the share of the budget devoted to national defense does not necessarily mean that defense outlays have actually fallen, but only that they have risen less rapidly than total outlays. In fact, however, dollar outlays for national defense did fall in ten of these thirty years. Expressed in constant 1969 dollars to compensate for the reduction in the purchasing power of the dollar, defense outlays fluctuated between $55 billion and $63 billion during fiscal years 1955 through 1966. Following a Vietnam-induced buildup to $83 billion in fiscal year 1968, in constant dollars, defense outlays fell more than $30 billion by fiscal year 1975 to a level of $51 billion, their lowest level since fiscal year 1951. Fiscal 1976 outlays remained at this level.[4]

Corresponding to the decreased importance of defense outlays in the budget is the greater importance of federal health and income security programs. With the introduction of medicare and medicaid in the mid-1960s, federal outlays for health (as a percent of total federal outlays) rose from less than 2 percent to 8 percent a decade later. (Reflecting these changes, the outlays of the Department of Health, Education, and Welfare surpassed those of the Defense Department in fiscal year 1971.)

Outlays for income security, including social security and unemployment insurance, drifted upward from 10 percent of total outlays in fiscal year 1948 to 15 percent in fiscal year 1957. Then, from fiscal years 1958 through 1970, they averaged about 20 percent of outlays. Following liberalization of unemployment compensation and increased social security and civil service retirement benefits, the figures began to rise again in fiscal year 1971, when income security programs accounted for more than a quarter of all outlays. In fiscal year 1976, outlays for income security amounted to one-third of all outlays. With social security and civil service retirement tied to the cost of living, the prospect is for further increases in these outlays.

Medicare and medicaid, social security, and unemployment compensation have several things in common. The most important is that they are all entitlement programs mandated by legislation (all but medicaid are financed through trust funds). Anyone who meets the criteria enumerated in the underlying legislation is entitled to receive benefits from these programs. During the normal budget review process, Congress has no discretion in determining how much to spend on these programs. Rather, Congress can only make an estimate of

4. Thomas J. Cuny and others, "The Budget in Constant Dollars," Technical Staff Paper (Office of Management and Budget, 1975; processed), p. 12.

the number of people who will claim benefits during the coming year and the amount of benefits that existing law provides for them. In a sense, these programs are uncontrollable. In precisely what sense they are uncontrollable and what can be done to increase their controllability will be discussed shortly. First, a look at federal revenue trends is in order to complement the picture of trends in outlays.

Trends in Federal Receipts

Trends in federal tax receipts are portrayed in table 4-1. Although total receipts have not paralleled outlays exactly—the government ran surpluses in some years, deficits in others—the general order of increase has been the same.

Until the Civil War, customs receipts were overwhelmingly the most important source of federal revenues, accounting for 90–95 percent of all receipts. The war years, however, saw a large increase in federal excise taxes, and excise taxes actually exceeded customs receipts in 1865 and 1866. Subsequently, customs receipts were again preeminent, but excise taxes remained a revenue source of major importance, contributing on the average about 35 percent of all federal receipts up to World War II.

The emergence of excise taxation marked a shift from external to internal revenue. This change gained momentum with the introduction of the individual and corporation income taxes in 1913 and 1909 respectively; by 1929 these two income taxes accounted for more than three-quarters of all federal tax receipts. Until 1943, the corporation income tax usually generated more revenue each year than the individual income tax. During World War II, however, the individual income tax was greatly expanded as a source of war revenue. Individual income tax receipts rose from $1.4 billion in 1941 to $19 billion just four years later. The corporation income tax, on the other hand, rose from $2.1 billion to $16 billion over the same period. The individual income tax has been the most productive single tax in the federal tax system since that time.

Of late, however, payroll taxes, introduced into the federal tax system by the Social Security Act of 1935, have grown markedly and contribute a substantial portion of total revenues produced. In recent years, as a matter of fact, most U.S. citizens have been paying more in social security taxes than they do in income taxes. In fiscal year

Table 4-1. Federal Receipts, Selected Fiscal Years, 1792–1976[a]

Fiscal year	Individual income taxes	Corporation income taxes	Excise taxes	Social insurance taxes and contributions	Estate and gift taxes	Customs duties	Other	Total
				Millions of dollars				
1792	...	...	...	...	...	3	*	4
1860	...	...	...	...	...	53	3	56
1910	...	34	267	...	...	334	41	676
1937	1,092	1,088	1,765	266	306	486	291	5,294
1968	68,726	28,665	14,079	34,622	3,051	2,038	2,491	153,671
1976	131,603	41,409	16,963	92,714	5,216	4,074	8,026	300,005
				Percentage of total				
1792	...	...	...	...	...	92	8	100
1860	...	...	...	...	...	95	5	100
1910	...	5	40	...	...	49	6	100
1937	21	21	33	5	6	9	5	100
1968	45	19	9	22	2	1	2	100
1976	44	14	6	31	2	1	3	100

Sources: 1792–1937, U.S. Bureau of the Census, *Historical Statistics of the United States, Colonial Times to 1970* (GPO, 1975), pt. 2, pp. 1106–09. Later years, *The Budget of the United States Government, Fiscal Year 1977*, pp. 358–59, and ibid., *Fiscal Year 1978*, pp. 424–25. Figures are rounded.
* Less than 0.5.
a. Data for 1792 are for the calendar year.

1976, social insurance taxes and contributions amounted to about $93 billion, or 31 percent of total tax revenues, compared with individual income tax receipts of $132 billion, or 44 percent of total revenues, and corporation income taxes of $41 billion, or 14 percent of the total.

The major trends that emerge from this brief consideration of federal revenues over the past 184 years are: (1) revenues have grown at just about the same pace as have outlays; (2) there has been a dramatic shift from external to internal revenue; and (3) income taxes (both individual and corporation) and payroll taxes today amount to about 90 percent of total federal revenues.

Deficits and Surpluses

Since 1792 the federal government has run deficits in eighty-three years and surpluses in one hundred and one years. The pattern of deficits and surpluses over this period is shown in figure 4-6. As is clear from the figure, the large deficits have for the most part been incurred in periods of war, although there have been a number of large nonwar deficits, notably those of the 1930s and the 1960s and 1970s.

Figure 4-6 also shows that deficits are not peculiar to the period since the 1930s, as is sometimes suggested. From 1792 to 1920, there were forty-six deficit years and eighty-two surplus years, or a deficit in roughly one out of three years. The ratio of deficit years is much higher, of course, for the more recent period: since 1930 there have been nine years of surpluses and thirty-seven years of deficits. There have been only eight surpluses in the twenty-nine years since World War II.

Since 1792 the deficits have been cumulatively greater than the surpluses, and thus the federal government has accumulated a sizable public debt. By the beginning of fiscal year 1977, the total federal debt was $631.9 billion.

Comparison of Estimated and Actual Budget Figures

Observers in the news media and politicians themselves often comment on the disparity between budget estimates of outlays, receipts, and deficits (or surpluses) and the outlays, receipts, and deficits that

Figure 4-6. Federal Deficits and Surpluses, 1792–1976a

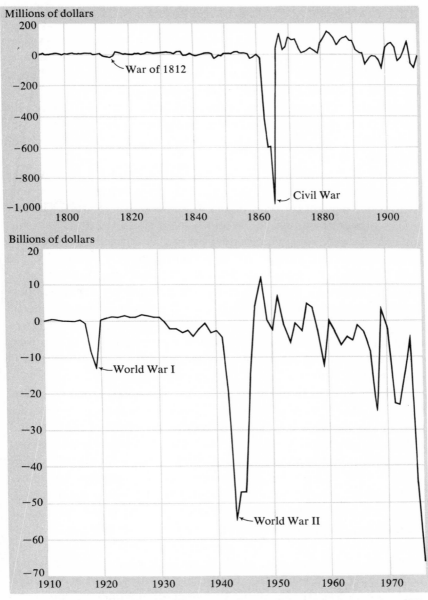

Sources: Data for 1792–1939 from Bureau of the Census, *Historical Statistics,* pt. 2, p. 1104. Data for 1940–76 from *The Budget of the United States Government, Fiscal Year 1978,* p. 437.

a. Calendar years through 1842; fiscal years ending June 30 beginning in 1844. Data for 1843 cover only the period January through June.

are actually realized. Frequently the implication is that budget estimates are not to be trusted or even that they are twisted for political purposes.

Table 4-2 shows estimated and actual receipts and outlays since fiscal year 1969. Receipts and outlays are both estimated twice in the budget. The first estimate for any fiscal year occurs in the budget document for that fiscal year, which is delivered to Congress about eight and a half months (beginning with fiscal year 1977) before the fiscal year begins. The second estimate is given in the following year's budget document, which appears about a third of the way through the fiscal year.

Table 4-2 shows that, during the period 1969–75, the average annual error—disregarding the sign of the error—of the first estimate averaged 2 percent for outlays and 4.7 percent for receipts. The second estimates of outlays and receipts, made when the fiscal year was under way, were somewhat better: the error averaged 1.6 percent of actual outlays and 2.5 percent of actual receipts. It is interesting to note that the first estimate of the *algebraic* averages of the errors—where underestimates tend to cancel overestimates—were a 1.8 percent overestimate of outlays and an 0.8 percent underestimate of receipts. Again, the second estimates were better: the second estimate of receipts averaged only two-tenths of a percentage point less than actual receipts, and the second estimate of outlays, on average, was equal to actual outlays.

Although errors in estimating receipts and outlays tend to cancel one another over a period of years, in any given year they can be quite large. How do these large errors develop? Forecasts of receipts and outlays involve predictions of international events and economic conditions for a twenty-one-month period; the budget submitted in mid-January 1977 was for the twelve-month period beginning the following October—almost nine months after the budget was submitted. In the period between the submission of the budget and the start of the fiscal year, or at any time during the fiscal year, international upheavals or unexpected changes in economic conditions at home can drastically alter expenditure needs or the basic assumptions on which receipts have been estimated. Furthermore, when there is a change in administrations, the incoming President often requests Congress to make substantial changes in the budget estimates submitted by the outgoing President. And finally, the Congress, during the congres-

Table 4-2. Actual and Estimated Budget Receipts and Outlays, Fiscal Years 1969–75

Amounts in billions of dollars

Fiscal year	Amount			Actual minus first estimate		Actual minus second estimate	
	First estimate	Second estimate	Actual	Amount	As percent of actual	Amount	As percent of actual
Receipts							
1969	178.1	186.1	187.8	9.7	5.2	1.7	0.9
1970	198.7	199.4	193.7	-5.0	-2.6	-5.7	-2.9
1971	202.1	194.2	188.4	-13.7	-7.3	-5.8	-3.1
1972	217.6	197.8	208.6	-9.0	-4.3	10.8	5.2
1973	220.8	225.0	232.2	11.4	4.9	7.2	3.1
1974	256.0	270.0	264.9	8.9	3.4	-5.1	-1.9
1975	295.0	278.7	281.0	-14.0	-5.0	2.3	0.8
Outlays							
1969	186.1	183.7	184.6	-1.5	-0.8	0.9	0.5
1970	195.3	197.9	196.6	1.3	0.7	-1.3	-0.7
1971	200.8	212.8	211.4	10.6	5.0	-1.4	-0.7
1972	229.2	236.6	231.9	2.7	1.2	-4.7	2.0
1973	246.3	249.8	246.5	0.2	0.1	-3.3	-1.3
1974	268.7	274.7	268.4	-0.3	-0.1	-6.3	-2.3
1975	304.4	313.4	324.6	20.2	6.2	11.2	3.4

Sources: *The Budget of the United States Government, Fiscal Year 1977*, p. 311, and preceding issues.

Table 4-3. Budget Receipts, Estimated and Actual, by Source, Fiscal Year 1975
Billions of dollars

Source	February 1974 estimate	Actual	Change, actual less estimate
Individual income taxes	129.0	122.4	−6.6
Corporation income taxes	48.0	40.6	−7.4
Social insurance taxes and contributions	85.6	86.4	0.8
Excise taxes	17.4	16.6	−0.9
Estate and gift taxes	6.0	4.6	−1.4
Customs	3.8	3.7	−0.1
Miscellaneous receipts	5.2	6.7	1.6
All receipts	295.0	281.0	−14.0

Source: *The Budget of the United States Government, Fiscal Year 1977*, p. 51.

sional budget review, may alter the President's budget program, with resulting substantial differences between requested and actual receipts and outlays.

While there is no need to belabor this issue, it is instructive to look at fiscal year 1975 receipts and compare them with the estimates in the fiscal 1975 budget. This comparison is shown in table 4-3. Receipts for fiscal year 1975 were originally estimated at $295 billion; actual receipts for the year were $14 billion lower than this estimate, largely because legislated tax changes were different from those assumed in the budget for the individual and corporation income taxes. The estimate of yields from the individual income tax in 1975 were $6.6 billion lower than had been anticipated; the major cause of this was the Tax Reduction Act of 1975, which reduced individual income tax receipts in 1975 by $9.4 billion. This reduction in tax receipts was partially offset by increases in tax receipts of $3.0 billion. About $1 billion of this resulted from congressional inaction on tax reform and simplification proposals in the 1975 budget, and $2.0 billion was due to a value of personal income higher than originally estimated in calendar year 1974.

Corporation income tax receipts were $7.4 billion lower than expected. The Tax Reduction Act of 1975 reduced receipts by $0.8 billion, while congressional inaction on a proposed windfall profits tax on the sale of domestic crude oil reduced them by $3.0 billion. The remaining $3.6 billion was due to an increase of $2.0 billion in refunds and a $1.6 billion reduction in tax payments. Social insurance taxes and contributions were $0.8 billion higher than estimated, with virtually all of the increase in higher unemployment taxes. Excise taxes, estate and gift taxes, and custom duties were somewhat below original estimates. Miscellaneous receipts were $1.6 billion higher than originally estimated primarily because of an underestimate of the earnings of the Federal Reserve System during the year and the increased import fees on petroleum products.

Controllability of Budget Outlays

With budget deficits having been incurred in twenty-one of the twenty-six years 1951–76, it is worth considering the extent to which budget outlays are uncontrollable. In what sense can a federal outlay be considered uncontrollable? A straightforward definition is as follows: "In any given fiscal year, an outlay is uncontrollable if it is mandated under an existing law or if it represents the liquidation of a contractual obligation of the government that was made prior to the start of the fiscal year in question."[5]

Examples of outlays that meet this definition are easy to come by. As indicated earlier in this chapter, medicare and medicaid, social security benefits, and unemployment compensation are mandated under existing legislation; these outlays are all uncontrollable. In the 1976 budget, uncontrollable federal payments of this sort to individuals amounted to $174 billion and outlays to liquidate obligations incurred in earlier years totaled $51 billion. Table 4-4 shows the controllability of federal outlays for selected recent fiscal years; in fiscal year 1976, three-quarters of all outlays are classified as relatively uncontrollable.

What is the significance of this kind of technical classification? Does it mean that nothing can be done to reduce three-fourths of the budget but that the other one-fourth is entirely discretionary? It does not.

It was estimated that roughly two-thirds of technically controllable outlays in 1976 were used for personnel compensation and benefits. Paring personnel costs, which is difficult enough for most private organizations, is nearly impossible for the federal government. As for the other third of "controllable" outlays, it was estimated that only

5. Barry M. Blechman, Edward M. Gramlich, and Robert W. Hartman, *Setting National Priorities: The 1976 Budget* (Brookings Institution, 1975), p. 192.

**Table 4-4. Federal Budget Outlays, by Controllability Category,
Fiscal Years 1968, 1972, 1976**

Category	1968	1972	1976
Billions of dollars			
Relatively uncontrollable under present law	**107.3**	**153.5**	**267.7**
Payments for individuals	47.7	88.4	174.4
Outlays from prior-year contracts and obligations	42.4	39.3	50.9
National defense	24.6	19.9	19.1
Civilian programs	17.8	19.4	31.8
Other	17.3	25.9	42.4
Relatively controllable	**73.4**	**81.1**	**103.0**
National defense	52.7	53.5	64.1
Civilian programs	20.7	27.7	38.8
Undistributed employer share, employee retirement	**−1.8**	**−2.8**	**−4.2**
Unified budget outlays, total	**178.8**	**231.9**	**366.5**
Percentage of unified budget outlays			
Relatively uncontrollable under present law	**60.0**	**66.2**	**73.1**
Payments for individuals	26.7	38.1	47.6
Outlays from prior-year contracts and obligations	23.7	16.9	13.9
National defense	13.8	8.6	5.2
Civilian programs	10.0	8.4	8.7
Other	9.7	11.2	11.6
Relatively controllable	**41.0**	**35.0**	**28.1**
National defense	29.5	23.1	17.5
Civilian programs	11.6	11.9	10.6
Undistributed employer share, employee retirement	**−1.0**	**−1.2**	**−1.2**
Unified budget outlays, total	**100.0**	**100.0**	**100.0**

Source: *The Budget of the United States Government, Fiscal Year 1978*, pp. 420–21. Figures are rounded.

about half could actually have been eliminated—mostly from defense procurement—and doing so would presuppose drastic policy shifts.[6]

Recall that the definition of controllability rests on "existing legislation" and "prior-year contracts." Congress can amend or repeal existing legislation and it can terminate outstanding contracts. Thus, it is somewhat misleading to describe any federal outlay as uncontrollable; Congress can reduce or eliminate any item in the budget. In fact, Congress has revised the underlying social security and medicare legislation to provide increased benefits nine times between 1970 and 1976 (see table 4-5). Although it would be politically difficult, Congress could reduce such outlays instead of increasing them.

The primary purpose for distinguishing between "controllable" and "uncontrollable" outlays, however, is to get some feel for the

6. See ibid., pp. 203–06.

Table 4-5. Major Changes in Social Security Benefits, 1970–76

Effective date	Type of change	Cost[a] (billions of dollars)
January 1970	15 percent OASDI[b] benefit increase and liberalization of benefits for various groups	4.4
January 1971	10 percent OASDI benefit increase	3.6
September 1972	20 percent OASDI benefit increase	8.5
January 1973	Substantial liberalization of benefits for various groups, especially widows and widowers	2.3
July 1973	Medicare benefits increased, including liberalization of benefits for various groups	2.0
March 1974	7 percent OASDI benefit increase	3.7
June 1974	4 percent OASDI benefit increase	2.1
June 1975	8 percent OASDI benefit increase	5.0
June 1976	6.4 percent OASDI benefit increase	5.0

Source: Social Security Administration.
a. Cost for the first twelve months following the effective date.
b. OASDI = old age, survivors, and disability insurance.

range within which federal outlays can be varied through the normal budget process. Making fundamental changes in federal programs in order to change outlays is a long-run process not usually carried out during any one budget year. In the new budget process (discussed in chapter 3), both the executive branch and the Congress are required to present five-year budget projections each year. This longer-term framework should provide the executive and Congress with a better means of assessing the impact of current budget decisions on future budgets and thus work toward reducing the uncontrollability of the federal budget.

Summary

Since 1792, federal spending has risen substantially in current and constant dollars as well as per capita. The rise in spending brought with it, especially during wars and recessions, large budget deficits. Since the cumulative deficits have excluded the cumulative surpluses, there is a large federal debt outstanding, amounting to $632 billion at the beginning of fiscal year 1977.

To some extent, budget deficits (or surpluses) are predictable, though errors occur when national or international conditions change so as to render inapplicable the assumptions underlying the estimates, especially the estimates of revenues. A substantial portion of the federal budget is mandated under existing legislation and is therefore technically "uncontrollable," and a considerable portion even of the "controllable" outlays is not really controllable either. Congress can reduce the "uncontrollability" of the budget by amending or repealing existing legislation. However, the likelihood of such action on most programs is small.

CHAPTER FIVE

Federal Budget Policy
and the Economy

SINCE the 1930s, it has been widely accepted that the federal budget can and should be used to level out the ups and downs of the economy—that is, that federal budget policy should be an important part of economic stabilization policy. In addition to its use as a stabilizing tool, the federal budget has been used to stimulate economic growth and to correct the imbalance in the nation's balance of payments.

This chapter discusses the impact of budget policy on the nation's economy and the ways in which this impact must be taken into consideration when decisions are made on specific expenditure and tax policies.

The federal budget makes its impact on the nation's economy largely through its effect on aggregate spending. Spending by consumers, businesses, and government (federal, state, and local) determines output, employment, prices, and the trade balance. The federal government, through its taxing and spending policies, can effect changes in aggregate spending. In fact, the government's policies affect the economy whether the government plans it or not, and an understanding of the effect is important when budget and taxing plans are formulated.

Planned Spending

The nation's output, or gross national product, is the sum of spending by consumers, businesses, and government on goods and services produced domestically (that is, excluding imports), plus foreigners' purchases of goods produced in this country.[1] Consumers consume goods and services, business spends on capital goods and inventories (investment), and government purchases goods from private industry and also purchases the services of its employees. For any period, total spending, including business spending on inventories, always equals output. So to be included in the total, goods must by definition have been sold to government, consumers, businesses, and foreign countries or else have gone into business inventories. But what makes the output level for any period what it is? What causes the level to change?

Suppose that for some selected output level the planned or desired spending of consumers, businesses, government, and foreigners are added up, including planned additions to or decreases in inventories. Suppose also that what these sectors want to buy or add to inventories just equals the assumed output level. Under these circumstances, employment and output will continue at the desired level. What happens if consumers, government, businesses, or foreigners decide to spend more than before? Then total spending (including inventory accumulation) will be greater than output. Businesses will experience an unplanned reduction in their inventories, and to rebuild them they will seek to increase production, at least where this is possible. A decline in planned spending will produce the opposite effect: an unplanned increase in business inventories, leading to a reduction in output. The crucial force determining the level of output, then, is planned spending by consumers, businesses, government, and foreigners.

1. More precisely, gross national product is the total value of all currently produced final goods and services in the economy for some particular period, whether they are sold at home or abroad. "Final" goods or services are those that do not enter into the production of other goods. The production of "intermediate" goods—those used in the production of other goods or services—is excluded from this measure of the final product of the nation. In the national income accounts investment goods are treated as final goods and not as intermediate goods. To obtain the value of total output in a given period, an estimate is made of the amount of each final good or service produced and this amount is multiplied by the market price of that good.

Planned spending is also the crucial force determining the level of employment and hence of unemployment, since employment of labor services tends to vary in the same direction as GNP. More output requires more hours of labor and lower output requires fewer hours.

The relation of planned spending to prices and growth involves yet another concept: "potential" or "full-employment" GNP. At any given time there is a maximum potential GNP that is consistent with full employment of the nation's labor supply. That is, given the size of the labor force, the average work-week and work-year, and the average productivity of labor per man-hour, there is a certain GNP that could be produced if all the labor force were employed (allowing for the usual frictional unemployment).[2] Full-employment GNP obviously does not remain unchanged with the passage of time. The labor force will grow if the number of workers entering it is great enough so that it will more than offset reductions in the work-week and work-year. Likewise, research and development and the addition of new capital equipment will raise labor productivity.[3]

Actual GNP in current dollars may equal full-employment GNP or be lower or higher. If planned spending is greater than output at full employment, there will be what is called an "inflationary gap" between planned spending and full-employment GNP, and prices will tend to rise. This effect is sometimes termed an "excess demand" inflation, indicating that at full employment or capacity output the money demand for goods and services is in excess of the demand required to purchase this output at current prices. Theories concern-

2. Not all unemployment should cause concern. There is always an irreducible minimum of frictional unemployment because the economy does not work perfectly. "Normal" unemployment results from job switching, from the fact that vacant jobs and available workers are not always in the same place at the same time, and so on. The term "unemployment" will, therefore, be used here to mean unemployment in excess of normal frictional unemployment. For more detail on the definition and measurement of frictional unemployment, see U.S. Bureau of Labor Statistics, "The Extent and Nature of Frictional Unemployment," in Study Paper 6, *Employment, Growth, and Price Levels,* Prepared for the Joint Economic Committee, 86:1 (GPO, 1959).

3. Full-employment GNP is calculated by multiplying the available labor supply by average labor productivity. The available labor supply is the total labor supply less frictional unemployment, in man-hours. Suppose, for example, that the available labor supply is 200 billion man-hours (100 million workers working 40 hours a week 50 weeks a year). Then, if average productivity per man-hour were $10, full-employment GNP would be $2,000 billion.

ing inflation are very complex, and the speed and duration of inflation will not be analyzed in detail here. The essential fact to note is that when planned spending exceeds full-employment GNP, prices and wages tend to rise. On the other hand, if planned spending is weak and actual GNP is clearly less than full-employment GNP, unemployment can be expected, since employment varies with output and output is less than the output required for full employment of the labor force. In this case there will be what is called a "deflationary gap."

The government can attack rising prices or unemployment by causing planned spending to vary. If the economy is bumping against full-employment GNP and prices and wages are rising, the government may seek to restrain planned spending. If the economy is below full-employment GNP, the government may seek to bolster spending. A policy affecting only planned spending, however, may not be sufficient to achieve stable prices and eliminate unemployment at the same time. As the economy moves close to full employment, there is an upward pressure on prices: plants are pushed to capacity, overtime and third-shift work becomes necessary, inexperienced workers must be hired, and unit costs thus tend to rise. In addition, unions are likely to press for increased wages, and sellers having monopoly power may be more inclined to raise prices than to stabilize them.

The relation between unemployment and inflation is illustrated graphically in figure 5-1. Several combinations of the rate of unemployment and the rate of price increases are shown on the curve in the figure. At point *A* the rate of price increase is almost zero, but the unemployment rate is 5 percent, which is a higher rate than can be accounted for by frictional unemployment. When the unemployment rate is 4 percent, as at *B*, there is no unemployment in excess of that usually considered frictional, but prices rise by some 0.5 percent a year. Any point on the curve represents a trade-off between either more unemployment and lower prices, or lower unemployment and higher prices.

Until recently the relation between unemployment and prices in the United States followed the trade-off curve shown in figure 5-1. When unemployment rates were high—around 5 or 6 percent—inflation stayed around a 1–2 percent rate per year. Only when the unemployment rate fell to 4 percent or below did prices begin to rise 4 or 5 percent. During the 1970s, however, this relationship began to de-

Figure 5-1. A Trade-off Curve of the Relation between Unemployment and Prices

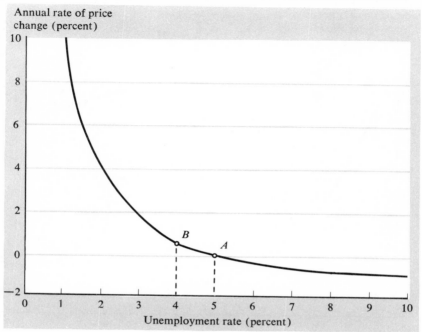

Annual rate of price change (percent)

Unemployment rate (percent)

teriorate. The trade-off curve shifted in an outward direction; that is, high rates of inflation and high rates of unemployment were in evidence.[4] Points like *D* and *E* in figure 5-2 describe the situation that prevailed in 1970 and 1974.

What happened to the trade-off during the period 1970–74? Several reasons have been suggested for the change in the economic relationships during this period. The major factors often cited are (1) the emergence of inflationary expectations that did not exist in the 1950s and 1960s;[5] (2) the devaluation of the dollar in early 1973, which led to a 24 percent increase in import prices over one year; (3) the worldwide food and raw materials shortages in 1973–74; (4) the

4. For a detailed analysis of the trade-off between unemployment and inflation (for the period 1956–74), see Barry M. Blechman, Edward M. Gramlich, and Robert W. Hartman, *Setting National Priorities: The 1976 Budget* (Brookings Institution, 1975), pp. 23–26.

5. As prices began to rise in the late 1960s, lenders, borrowers, businesses, and labor, in anticipation of further price increases, began to demand higher prices for their services. This behavior itself became an inflationary force causing prices and wages to rise more than they would have otherwise.

Figure 5-2. Trade-off between Inflation and Unemployment, 1960 and 1970–76ᵃ

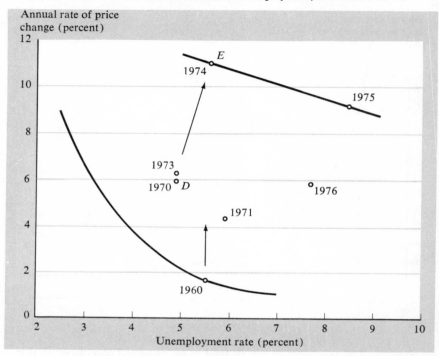

Sources: Inflation and unemployment rates from *Economic Report of the President, January 1977*, pp. 221, 241; and U.S. Bureau of Labor Statistics.
a. Does not include 1972 because wage and price controls were in effect during the year.

fourfold increases in world petroleum prices from mid-1973 to 1974; and (5) large budget deficits in the mid-1960s and in the 1970s.[6] The movement of the 1976 point to the left of the 1974–75 trade-off in figure 5-2 doubtless reflects the temporary muting of these factors.

Before discussing federal budget policy in situations where inflation and recession coexist, the role of the budget in the "normal" framework, where either inflation or excess unemployment exists, but not both, is examined.

6. In his testimony before the Senate Committee on the Budget, Secretary William E. Simon argued that there has been a close correspondence between the rate of inflation and the budget position. However, during the periods 1950–51 and 1973–74, the budget position was not sufficient to explain the prevailing rates of inflation. See Treasury Secretary William Simon's testimony in *The Federal Budget and Inflation*, Hearings before the Senate Committee on the Budget, 93:2 (GPO, 1974), p. 190.

Federal Budget Policy and Planned Spending

The government can exert considerable influence on spending—and thus on prices, employment, and output—by adjusting its expenditures or taxes, that is, by its use of fiscal policy. The responsibility for fiscal policy in the United States lies with the federal government. Although all levels of government—federal, state, and local—engage in making budgets and thus are engaged in budget policy, only the budgetary decisions of the federal government are large enough to have an extensive impact on the economy as a whole. In addition, it is difficult for a state or local government alone to pursue a policy designed to affect employment or prices, since neighboring states or localities may pursue opposing policies.

Since interest in this chapter is in federal fiscal policy—the way the federal budget affects the economy—the budget referred to is the national income budget, which (1) includes receipts and expenditures of trust funds, (2) excludes purely credit transactions, and (3) generally treats tax receipts on an accrual basis and expenditures on a delivery basis.

The Use of Fiscal Policy

The federal government affects planned spending by changing its own spending on goods and services and by causing consumer and business spending on goods and services to change by affecting consumer and business income. First, what causes private spending to change?

Private planned spending is affected by several factors. One of these, which receives particular emphasis at the working level of public policy, is the relation of private spending to private disposable income. Private disposable income is the income available for spending on goods and services by consumers and business firms after taxes. Consumer spending varies directly with disposable income; that is, the higher the disposable income, all other things being equal, the higher will be consumer spending.

Private spending is also affected by other forces, in particular by the liquidity of businesses and households,[8] terms of lending and

7. For a more detailed discussion of the national income budget, see pp. 10–12.

8. Liquidity is a measure of the extent to which consumers' and businesses' wealth are cash or assets readily convertible to cash.

credit conditions, and expectations concerning future income and prices. When expectations, credit conditions and terms of lending, or the liquidity of businesses and households change, planned spending for all levels of private disposable income is affected. For example, if businesses and consumers suddenly become more optimistic than they have been, they will plan to spend more of their disposable income; if they become more pessimistic, they will plan to spend less. If firms' and consumers' holdings become more liquid, perhaps because of an increase in their cash holdings, their spending will increase at all levels of disposable income, while if they become less liquid, their spending will decline. Finally, if credit is tightened or interest rates rise, private planned spending at all levels of disposable income can be expected to fall, while if credit is loosened or interest rates fall, private planned spending at all levels of disposable income can be expected to rise.

Even if expectations, liquidity, and credit conditions are given, federal budget action can affect private planned spending by changing the level of private disposable income. If the federal government reduces the amount it takes out of the GNP in taxes, consumers and businesses will be left with larger disposable incomes. This will encourage more private spending and the demand for output will rise. Likewise, if the federal government increases taxes, this will reduce disposable income, reduce private spending, and cause the demand for output to fall. Alternatively, the federal government can affect private disposable income by changes in federal spending on goods and services. Increased federal spending results in added income for someone. The industries receiving orders for federal goods have greater incomes and pay more wages to their labor forces than they would in the absence of these orders. With more income, businesses and consumers spend more.

Thus the federal government can affect private spending by changing private disposable income, either by changing taxes or by changing federal spending. The precise effects of these changes and combinations of the two will be considered below.

Effects of Changes in Federal Spending

Suppose the federal government reduces its purchases of goods and services without changing tax rates. How will this affect the economy? Other things being equal, lower expenditures by the federal government have a contractionary effect; that is, they tend to lower output and employment. Higher government purchases, on the other hand, have an expansionary effect; they tend to increase output and employment.

Suppose that GNP is $2,000 billion and is equal to planned spending, so that there is no tendency for GNP to change. Suppose also that consumers and businesses together spend 65 percent of any increase in private disposable income (60 percent on domestic goods and 5 percent on imported goods), so that each $1 change in private disposable income changes consumption and investment (including imports of goods) by 65 cents. Finally, suppose that government taxes away 20 percent of any increase in GNP, that the federal budget is balanced, and that there is no deficit or surplus in the balance of payments. If federal purchases of goods and services are permanently reduced by $10 billion (as a result of, say, a reduction in purchases of missiles or submarines, construction of new government buildings, or the number of government employees), output will fall by $19.2 billion, or almost twice the decrease in government spending; at the same time, a surplus of almost $1 billion will arise in the balance of payments.

Why does a reduction in government spending cause a multiple reduction in output and improve the balance of payments? When the government spends $10 billion less (and keeps its spending at the new lower level), GNP, or output, will first fall by the amount of goods and services, or output, the government would have purchased (assuming it would have been purchased domestically). As the $10 billion of income is lost by consumers and business firms, they will reduce expenditures on investment and consumption, and GNP will fall further. Under the assumptions we have made, out of each dollar of income lost as purchases fall, 20 cents will represent the reduction in taxes paid; after-tax incomes will fall by 80 cents. Consumers and firms will thus reduce their spending on domestic goods by 48 cents (that is, 60 percent of 80 cents). So each dollar of income lost will, according to the basic spending assumption, reduce private domestic spending by 48 cents. GNP will fall initially by $10 billion because of the decrease in government purchases; the loss in income will induce a decline in private domestic spending of $4.8 billion. This fall in spending will reduce private domestic spending by an additional $2.3 billion (60 percent of $3.8 billion, the fall in private disposable

Figure 5-3. Effect on GNP of a $10 Billion Decrease in Federal Purchases

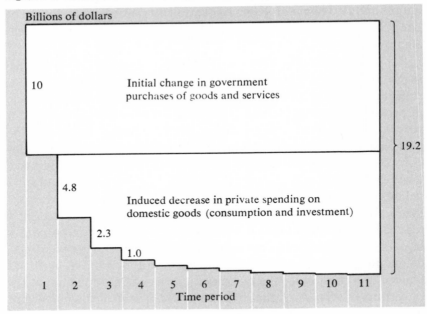

income after allowing for the $1 billion fall in taxes paid), and so on until a total change in GNP of $19.2 billion is reached, as shown in figure 5-3: $10 billion less of government purchases of goods and services and $9.2 billion less of private spending on domestic goods. At the same time, output of domestic goods is reduced, purchases of imports are also reduced; some 5 percent of each reduction in disposable income is reflected in a reduction in imports. Imports will thus fall by $768 million.

The whole process is reversed when there is an increase in government purchases of goods and services. GNP will rise by 1.92 times the increase in government purchases of goods and services and imports will rise by 5 percent of the increase in GNP.

Several qualifications need to be made at this point. The net contractionary effects of a permanent reduction in federal government spending may be moderated if private or state and local government expenditures are substituted for those that would otherwise have been undertaken. If, for example, the federal government has been absorbing investment opportunities open to the private sector, private investment outlays may rise when government spending falls, and this will counteract the restrictive effect of the decrease. The contractionary effect will also be moderated if part or all of the decrease in government purchases is in imported goods and services. In this case, the direct effect of the reduced federal purchases on domestic output will be offset by the amount that would have been spent on foreign goods, and thus the multiplier effect of a decrease in expenditures will be reduced.

The monetary aspects of the fiscal action may also alter the total effect of the decrease or increase in federal spending. A reduction in government expenditures cuts total planned spending and at the same time the demand for money. If no corresponding reduction in the supply of money is forthcoming, there will be downward pressures on interest rates. Business investment as well as those consumer expenditures that are sensitive to changes in the interest rate will be increased, partially offsetting the contractionary effect of the fiscal action.[9] Similarly, an increase in government spending increases aggregate planned spending and the demand for money. With unchanged supply of money, this increment in government spending will push interest rates upward, thus inducing a reduction in investment and consumer spending. The expansionary effect of the fiscal action will be reduced.

However, reductions in government spending on goods and services are generally contractionary, and increases have a stimulative effect. If there is slack in the economy, an increase in spending will generally cause output to rise. If the economy is nearer (or at) full employment, an increase may bring about some increase in real output but most certainly will cause prices to rise.[10]

Effects of Changes in Taxes

Assuming that everything else (including government expenditures) remains the same, an increase in federal tax rates means less private disposable income, and this in turn means less private spending. Whatever the level of GNP, a tax increase will therefore tend to reduce output (GNP) and imports because it will reduce private

9. These monetary effects are discussed in more detail in chapter 6.

10. Also, increases in government spending tend to increase imports, while reductions in government spending tend to reduce them. The resulting deficit or surplus in the balance of trade will be offset by movements in the exchange rate under a floating system of exchange rates. Since the exchange rate is now allowed to float, the effect of fiscal action on the balance of payments may be disregarded.

spending. A tax cut, on the other hand, will tend to raise output (assuming output below full employment output) and imports by raising private spending.[11]

Suppose the situation is the same as in the example of the effects of a reduction in government spending given earlier (pages 80–82). Suppose that with GNP at $2,000 billion the federal government decides to raise tax rates. Specifically, suppose a rise in tax rates is planned so that, if GNP stays at $2,000 billion, tax revenues will rise by $10 billion. This could be accomplished by raising the fraction of GNP that is taken by taxes from 20 percent to 20.5 percent; the higher rate would bring in $10 billion additional revenue.

The effect of this $10 billion tax increase will be to cause the level of GNP to fall by $11.3 billion, or 1.13 times the tax increase of $10 billion. The process is similar to what happens in the case of a government expenditure decrease. The increase in taxes will initially take away $10 billion of disposable income from the private sector. This fall in disposable income will cause the private sector to spend $6 billion less on domestic goods (60 percent of $10 billion). The reduction in spending will generate a further fall in income of $6 billion, of which $4.72 billion constitutes a reduction in spending on domestic goods and about $1.28 billion a reduction in tax revenues. As private spending is reduced by $4.72 billion, income will fall by the same amount. This fall in income will be reflected in another reduction in spending by the private sector: 60 percent of $4.72 billion, or $2.83 billion. Income will again automatically fall by an equal amount, and the process will be repeated until the total decrease of $11.3 billion has been reached. The fall in private incomes will also

11. Changes in certain types of government expenditures have the same effect on GNP as tax changes in that they change private disposable income without changing government purchases of goods and services. The most important of these at the federal level are interest payments on the federal debt and transfer payments. The latter consist of payments made to individuals where no service is rendered, such as unemployment compensation and old-age benefits. Reductions in transfer payments or (net) interest payments are comparable to increases in taxes, since they also reduce private disposable income. Increases in transfer payments or (net) interest payments have the same effect as tax cuts; that is, they increase private disposable income.

Hence, throughout our discussion in this chapter we use the terms "expenditure changes" loosely to mean changes in purchases of goods and services and "tax changes" to mean changes in transfer and interest payments as well as tax changes narrowly defined.

cause imports to fall, thus increasing the surplus or reducing the deficit in the balance of payments.

Note that although a tax increase of $10 billion was assumed, actual tax revenues will not rise by this amount. The $10 billion increase was based on the old level of GNP ($2,000 billion). But since the tax increase will cause GNP to fall, the increase in revenue will be partially offset by the fall in GNP. The fall in GNP of $11.3 billion will induce a fall in tax receipts of 20.5 percent of the change in GNP, or some $2.3 billion. The net effect of the tax increase will be to reduce the deficit (or increase the surplus) by only $7.7 billion, not by the original $10 billion.

This discrepancy will also occur in the case of the government expenditure decrease mentioned earlier. Because the reduction will induce a fall in GNP, tax revenues will also fall. The fall in GNP will cause tax revenues to fall by an amount equal to $3.84 billion (that is, 20 percent of the $19.2 billion decrease in GNP), which will be a partial offset to the $10 billion reduction in government expenditures, and the deficit will be reduced by only $6.16 billion.[12]

Achieving the Domestic Goal of Full-Employment GNP by Changing Expenditures and Taxes

Assume that the economy is under inflationary pressure and that the money demand for output exceeds output at full employment. Under these conditions, five combinations of tax and expenditure changes can be used to match planned spending and full-employment output. The federal government can: (1) reduce its purchases of goods and services without changing tax rates; (2) increase tax rates without changing its purchases; (3) simultaneously reduce spending

12. Again it should be emphasized that this analysis of the effects of taxes on GNP ignores the effects on spending of changes in money or other assets held by the public as a result of deficits or surpluses in the government budget. As long as the government runs a deficit, net assets held by the public (money or government securities) will increase, and this will tend to raise private spending apart from the effects on income of tax and expenditure changes. The relationship holds in the opposite direction as well: as long as the government runs a surplus, there will be a downward pressure on private demand apart from changes in income. For a more complete discussion of this point, see David J. Ott and Attiat F. Ott, "Budget Balance and Equilibrium Income," *Journal of Finance*, vol. 20 (March 1965), pp. 71–77, and Alan S. Blinder and Robert M. Solow, "Analytical Foundations of Fiscal Policy," in Blinder and others, *The Economics of Public Finance* (Brookings Institution, 1974), pp. 47–55.

and raise tax rates; (4) reduce both spending and taxes; (5) raise spending and increase taxes.

To illustrate some of these possibilities, suppose that, in the earlier example, the demand for GNP (measured at current prices) is $50 billion greater than full-employment GNP (also measured at current prices). How large a reduction in government spending will it take to lower GNP by $50 billion? Under the assumptions made earlier about the percentage change in income spent and the additional percentage of GNP taken by taxes, for every dollar reduction in government spending, GNP will tend to fall by $1.92. If GNP is to fall by $50 billion as a result of a change in government spending alone, the required change can be calculated by dividing $50 billion by 1.92, obtaining $26 billion. This method of reducing GNP will increase the budget surplus or reduce the deficit by $16 billion. The fall of $50 billion in GNP will reduce tax revenue by $10 billion (20 percent of $50 billion), which will partially offset the decrease of $26 billion in expenditures.

Now suppose that, under the same conditions, the federal government attempts to reduce GNP by $50 billion by increasing tax rates alone. The necessary dollar tax increase, at the old GNP level, can be calculated by dividing $50 billion by 1.13 (the tax multiplier) to obtain $44.2 billion. At the old GNP of $2,000 billion, this would mean an increase in tax rates from 20 percent to 22.2 percent of GNP, or by 2.2 percentage points. The effect of the government's budget position in this case would be to increase the surplus or reduce the deficit by $33.1 billion; the $44.2 billion rise in taxes would be offset partially by an $11.1 billion fall in taxes (22.2 percent of $50 billion) resulting from the decrease of $50 billion in GNP.

Thus, to achieve the same reduction in GNP, the required dollar tax increase would be larger than the required cut in government purchases of goods and services. This result comes about because the government expenditure multiplier is larger than the tax multiplier. It should also be noted that, because of the larger size of the tax increase required to achieve the same change in GNP, the tax increase would have a greater impact on the surplus or deficit of the government. The reduction in government purchases would increase the surplus or reduce the deficit by $16 billion, whereas the tax increase achieving the same reduction in GNP would increase the surplus or reduce the deficit by $33.1 billion.

The government can also close the gap between actual and full-employment GNP by policies combining in various ways reductions in purchases of goods and services and increases in taxes. For example, if, to achieve a reduction of $50 billion in GNP, it was decided to reduce government purchases of goods and services by $10 billion, this alone would reduce GNP by about $19.2 billion; the tax increase needed to produce the remaining $30.8 billion reduction in GNP would be $27.3 billion ($30.8 billion divided by 1.13). Similarly, other combinations of taxes and purchases might be used to accomplish a $50 billion reduction in GNP.

Finally, GNP can be reduced by cutting government purchases and taxes equally, that is, by *balanced* reductions in government purchases and taxes. If a dollar change in government purchases affects GNP more than a dollar change in taxes, then clearly a $1 reduction of government purchases will reduce GNP more than a $1 reduction in taxes will raise GNP. That is, although lower spending by government lowers GNP and lower taxes raise GNP, the expenditure change has more impact than the tax change, and on balance GNP will fall when government expenditures and taxes are reduced equally. Thus, equal reductions in government spending and taxes can be planned to close the gap between the demand for GNP and full-employment GNP. In short, balanced budget changes are not inconsistent with the use of expenditure and tax policy to maintain full employment and price stability.

The example given above dealt with an inflationary situation. One could have chosen the opposite case where planned spending was below what is required to maintain full-employment GNP. In this case fiscal action would be needed to increase planned spending. This could be done by increasing government purchases, by reducing taxes, by increasing government purchases *and* reducing taxes, or by increasing both government purchases and taxes. The conclusion reached above on the necessary changes in government purchases and taxes and the effects on the budget would simply be reversed in this situation.

It should be recognized that in actual practice the effects of tax and expenditure policy might not work out exactly as described here. There might be changes in expenditures or in other circumstances that would cause the relation of spending and income to vary and thus alter the final outcome. This discussion has assumed that "all other things have been equal."

Fiscal Policy Options When Inflation and Recession Coexist

The coexistence of inflation and recession complicates the discussion of the direction fiscal policy ought to take. For example, if inflation were the only problem, fiscal restraint—an increase in taxes, a cut in federal spending, or both—would be called for. If achieving full employment were the target, an expansionary fiscal policy could inject the needed stimulus to eliminate unemployment. When both unemployment and inflation coexist, it is not at all clear whether a policy of restraint should be preferred to a stimulatory policy or vice versa, inasmuch as neither policy can accomplish both objectives simultaneously. A choice must be made as to the relative importance of price stability and full employment as goals. In such a setting there is no escaping the trade-off. The choice of the appropriate budget posture will hinge on the weights policymakers attach to each of these two goals and on their expectations about the response of economic variables to the policy choices. Some policymakers may opt for an expansionary fiscal policy, because they believe the unemployment problem to be more critical than the danger of inflation. Others may see the issue differently. They see great danger in allowing inflation to go unchecked, even if it is necessary to tolerate a higher level of unemployment. According to this view, allowing the economy to cool off is more important for long-run stability than reducing unemployment, since reducing unemployment will only trigger additional rounds of inflation (and perhaps unemployment).

In short, when conflicting goals exist, fiscal policy alone cannot achieve all of them.

The Deficit or Surplus as a Measure of Fiscal Policy

Popular discussion of the effect of the budget on the economy in the press, in Congress, and even to some extent among economists often focuses on the current budget deficit or surplus. It is said that when the federal government runs a deficit the effect on the economy is expansionary, and when it runs a surplus the effect is restrictive. As a matter of fact, the actual federal government surplus or deficit reveals nothing about the "tightness" or "looseness" of the government's fiscal program, and using it as an indicator often leads to wrong conclusions.

Government deficits or surpluses are poor guides for interpreting fiscal policy because they reflect not only the decisions of Congress on spending and tax rates (discretionary fiscal action) but also the response of tax revenues and transfer payments to changes in GNP. Even with no change in tax rates or expenditures, the federal deficit or surplus varies as GNP varies. The federal deficit may increase because GNP falls (tax revenues fall and transfer payments rise), or it may increase as a result of discretionary action (a tax cut or an increase in expenditures). The resulting deficits are not the same in their economic impact: one occurs as a result of a fall in GNP (with no change in budget policy), while the other is created to help produce an increase in GNP. Since the impact in the two cases cannot be equated, the size of the federal deficit cannot be a reliable measure of fiscal policy.

To remedy these defects, the concept of a *full-employment budget* was developed. The full-employment budget is an estimate of what the federal surplus or deficit would be if the economy were operating at full employment. It separates the effects of changes in the federal government tax and expenditure policy from the effects of changes in the level of economic activity.

Although the concept dates back to the immediate postwar period in the proposal made by the Committee for Economic Development in 1947, it became popular as a fiscal planning tool during the early 1960s when it was explained in detail in the 1962 annual report of the Council of Economic Advisers.

The full-employment budget concept may be clarified by reference to figure 5-4. Line G in the figure represents government spending, assumed to be independent of the level of GNP. Taxes are represented by line T. It is positively sloped, reflecting the progressivity of the U.S. tax structure. Beginning with a GNP level of Y_o, the actual federal budget would show a deficit equal to the distance AB, which is the difference of government spending at Y_o and tax receipts generated at the output level Y_o.

Since Y_f, full-employment output, lies to the right of Y_o, comparing tax receipts at full employment with government spending shows a budget surplus of CD, the full-employment surplus. It arises because

Figure 5-4. Measuring Budget Impact

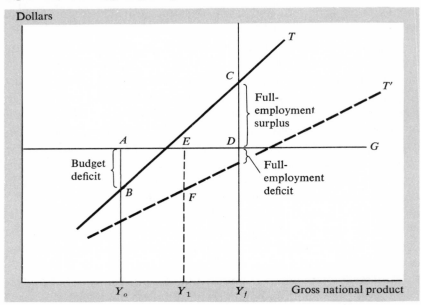

at the full-employment level of output, line T (given tax rates and the level of G) generates a high level of receipts and thus the full-employment surplus.

Suppose taxes are cut to get the economy moving toward full employment (from its Y_o position to Y_f). This would shift the T line to the right to T'; output rises from Y_o to Y_1 due to the discretionary fiscal action, and the full-employment budget surplus turns into a deficit. What about the size of the actual deficit or surplus? As shown in the figure, the actual budget still shows a deficit, but as output expands from Y_o to Y_1, the size of the actual deficit remains the same ($EF = AB$ by construction). If the expansion of output were to exceed Y_1, the deficit would be reduced. The fiscal action taken by the federal government will have turned the full-employment budget from a surplus to a deficit position; the lower tax rate T' generates tax receipts at full employment that fall short of general spending at full employment.

Since actual budget deficits may remain unaffected or even decline with expansionary fiscal action, the size of the actual deficit (or surplus) is not a useful measure of fiscal impact. Smaller deficits or larger surpluses are usually regarded as contractionary. Yet, as shown in figure 5-4, although the policy that moved the economy from Y_o to Y_1 was expansionary (as may be ascertained by looking at what happened to the full-employment surplus), the actual deficit was unaffected.

The standard calculation for the full-employment surplus is based on an assumed level of real GNP equal to "potential GNP." Full-employment expenditures are estimated to be equal to actual expenditures, with an adjustment for unemployment compensation benefits to reflect the fact that, as the level of unemployment falls when the economy moves toward potential GNP, unemployment benefits fall. Full-employment receipts are estimated at the full-employment level of GNP, given unchanged tax laws.

The full-employment surplus or deficit then measures the balance between revenues and expenditures at full-employment GNP. The actual surplus or deficit reflects both the automatic responses of taxes and expenditures to deviations of GNP from its full-employment rate as well as discretionary changes in taxes and expenditures. In table 5-1, actual budget deficits or surpluses in the national income accounts are compared with the full-employment deficits or surpluses for the period of 1968–76. As the table shows, the full-employment budget dramatically swung from a $33.5 billion deficit in the fourth quarter of 1972 to a $20.4 billion surplus in the third quarter of 1974. It then turned to a deficit of $37 billion by the second quarter of 1975. The move from deficit to surplus to deficit shows a reversal of policy from expansion to restraint, then to expansion during 1972–75. Similar shifts in policy also occurred during 1968–69: the full-employment budget turned from a $19.9 billion deficit in the second quarter of 1968 into a $5.0 billion surplus in the second quarter of 1969. In both cases the restrictive shifts in policy action contributed to the recession that followed.

Summary and Conclusion

This chapter has considered the impact of federal spending and taxation on the output of the economy, or GNP. Reductions in government purchases of goods and services are contractionary, while reductions in tax rates (or increases in transfer payments) are expansionary; since imports vary with GNP, contractionary fiscal ac-

Table 5-1. Actual and Full-Employment Federal Budget Surpluses or Deficits, Seasonally Adjusted Quarterly Totals at Annual Rates, 1968–76

Billions of dollars

Year and quarter	Actual	Full employment
1968:1	−9.7	−15.5
2	−12.0	−19.9
3	−2.3	−11.5
4	0.7	−7.5
1969:1	11.2	3.3
2	12.0	5.0
3	6.7	2.2
4	4.2	4.2
1970:1	−1.1	3.8
2	−12.8	−5.5
3	−14.6	−5.2
4	−20.1	−3.6
1971:1	−18.5	−6.1
2	−23.8	−11.6
3	−23.4	−10.0
4	−22.2	−8.9
1972:1	−13.4	−14.3
2	−20.0	−22.6
3	−10.8	−15.6
4	−24.9	−33.5
1973:1	−9.7	−13.3
2	−6.6	−9.1
3	−5.2	−5.5
4	−5.3	−3.7
1974:1	−4.1	5.2
2	−7.6	12.5
3	−9.0	20.4
4	−25.3	18.2
1975:1	−49.8	12.0
2	−99.9	−37.1
3	−66.0	−10.0
4	−69.4	−14.7
1976:1	−63.8	−14.1
2	−54.1	−6.7
3	−57.4	−8.2

Sources: Actual, U.S. Bureau of Economic Analysis, *The National Income and Product Accounts of the United States, 1929–74: Statistical Tables* (GPO, 1977), table 3.2; *Survey of Current Business*, vol. 56 (July 1976), table 3.2, and vol. 57 (January 1977), table 3.2. Full employment, Council of Economic Advisers. Full-employment estimates here assume lower productivity growth than is assumed in figure 2-1 and tables 2-4 and A-8.

tions improve the balance of payments and expansionary fiscal actions worsen the balance of payments. Per dollar, changes in government spending on goods and services are more potent in their effect on GNP than are changes in tax rates or transfer payments.

The impact of fiscal actions on GNP depends on the sensitivity to interest rates of the public's demand for liquid assets and private expenditures. The less responsive the public's demand for liquid assets and the more responsive private expenditures are to interest rate changes, the smaller the impact of changes in government expenditures or taxes.

Actual budget deficits or surpluses reflect both the responses of taxes and transfers to changes in GNP and discretionary changes in tax rates and spending. Thus, actual budget deficits or surpluses are not adequate measures of changes in fiscal policy. For this purpose, the full-employment surplus has been developed and widely used. The automatic responses of taxes and transfers (automatic stabilizers) to changes in GNP as well as the limitations of fiscal policy in achieving domestic goals of full employment and price stability are taken up in the next chapter.

CHAPTER SIX

Fiscal Policy
and the Budget Program

BY VARYING either expenditures or taxes, or both, the federal government can work toward simultaneous low unemployment and price stability. With fluctuating exchange rates, balance of payments equilibrium is automatically ensured.

By combining fiscal actions with appropriate monetary policy, the federal government can achieve its goals of internal and external balance and it can do this and have a balanced budget, a surplus, or a deficit. Several questions now arise. How successful is fiscal action? What reliance should be placed on the so-called automatic fiscal stabilizers? And what is the appropriate budget balance?

Restraints on Expenditures and Tax Changes: Lags in Fiscal Policy

The success of fiscal policy is hampered by the existence of certain lags in the economy. For fiscal or monetary policy to achieve its goals the policymaker must accurately forecast the economic event (recession or inflation) needing the action. He must know the length of time it takes for a policy to be put in effect and how fast the economy responds to alternative policy measures.

Economists have identified three types of fiscal policy lags: the recognition lag, the policy lag, and the outside lag. The recognition lag consists of the time between the occurrence of an economic event (say, the beginning of a recession) and the realization by the policy-makers that an action is needed. This lag exists because economic data take time to collect, verify, and analyze.[1] The recognition lag is, however, relatively short and therefore not a problem.

The policy lag is the time between the recognition of need for an action and the action itself. The speed with which policies may be changed is determined by political as well as technical considerations. Political characteristics of the United States make the lag shorter for expenditure changes than for taxes. Although changes in appropriations and tax changes must be legislated by Congress, the President can, to a limited extent, vary the rate of expenditure during a given period through apportionment of appropriations (see chapter 3). When tax changes are contemplated, there is no way to predict the size of the policy lag. It can be short (the Revenue Act of 1975 was enacted within four months of initiation) or it can be long. The lengthy legislative battle over the Revenue Act of 1962, which extended over a period of eighteen months, provides evidence that this lag can be very long.

Finally, the outside lag is the time which elapses from the beginning of a policy change to the attainment of the desired results. The size of the outside lag depends on the way the government sector is interrelated with the private sector. Several estimates of the size of this lag have been made with the aid of macroeconomic models of the economy.[2] The results reported in these studies suggest that at least 75 percent of the ultimate effect of a sustained increment in govern-

1. There are various indicators for checking the health of the economy, such as the "leading," "coincident," and "lagging" indicators published by the Department of Commerce and its quarterly estimates of gross national product, and the monthly unemployment data and monthly price indexes for consumer and wholesale goods published by the Department of Labor. These indicators still lag one month or one quarter from the time of the change in the economic event.

2. For a discussion of the empirical evidence and the model used in estimating the size of the outside lag, see Alan S. Blinder and Robert M. Solow, "Analytical Foundations of Fiscal Policy," in Blinder and others, *The Economics of Public Finance* (Brookings Institution, 1974), pp. 79–83.

ment spending is felt within the first year after the fiscal action is initiated.[3]

The uncertainties of forecasting and the existence of a somewhat lengthy policy lag have often been cited to support proposals aiming at improving the countercyclical power of the federal government. At various times, proposals have been made for Congress to give the President standby authority to cut taxes temporarily and to initiate public works programs to combat unemployment. Examples of such proposals are those made by the Commission on Money and Credit and the Committee for Economic Development.[4] Congress has not granted any of these requests and does not seem likely to do so in the near future.[5]

Automatic Fiscal Stabilizers

The automatic tax or expenditure changes built into the federal budget serve to cushion private disposable income when GNP changes. By so doing, they moderate the fall of private spending when GNP falls and limit the increase in private spending when GNP rises. As a result, GNP falls and rises less than it might otherwise because of their stabilizing effect. These stabilizers are automatic in the sense that they become effective when the level of GNP changes and do not require any decisions by the executive or Congress.

The two major fiscal stabilizers of the federal government are: (1) transfer payments, which are paid by the federal government to the aged, the poor, the unemployed, and other needy people in the nation; and (2) the personal and corporation income taxes and social security taxes.

Transfer payments vary inversely with GNP: as GNP rises, they

3. Ibid., p. 81.
4. *Review of Report of the Commission on Money and Credit,* Hearings before the Joint Economic Committee, 87:1 (GPO, 1961), p. 467; Committee for Economic Development, *Fiscal and Monetary Policy for High Employment* (CED, 1962), pp. 32–35.
5. One possibility open to the Congress is to enact a tax adjustment bill each year for the following calendar year to meet the needs of the economy. Such a procedure would fit well with the new budget process and protect the legislature's authority over tax matters. On this point, see *The Budget and the Economy: The Outlook for Calendar Years 1976 and 1977,* Report of the Task Force on Economic Projections to the House Committee on the Budget (GPO, 1976), pp. 22–23.

fall, and as GNP falls, they rise. For the most part, this is a reflection of the behavior of unemployment compensation, which rises when GNP falls (since unemployment increases) and falls when GNP rises. If, for example, a decline in private spending causes GNP to fall, rising unemployment compensation payments will moderate the fall of private disposable income. This will prevent consumer spending from falling sharply and check the fall in GNP. In addition, the federal tax structure has a stabilizing effect. As income increases, the ratio of taxes to income increases, and as income falls, the ratio falls. These automatic stabilizers have become an important force in the present-day U.S. economy. For every dollar that GNP declines during a downturn of the economy, the budget deficit rises by an estimated 25–30 cents, thereby limiting the decline.

The importance of these automatic stabilizers in maintaining disposable personal income when GNP falls is illustrated in figure 6-1, which shows changes in GNP and disposable personal income by quarters for 1961–76. As can be seen, the fluctuations in disposable

Figure 6-1. Quarterly Changes in Gross National Product and Disposable Income, 1961–76

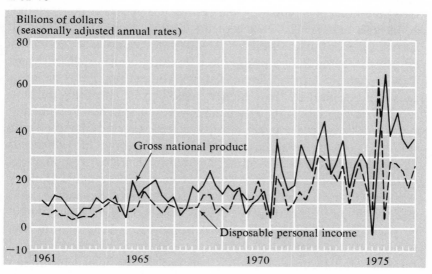

Sources: U.S. Bureau of Economic Analysis, *The National Income and Product Accounts of the United States, 1929–74: Statistical Tables* (GPO, 1977), tables 1.1, 2.1; *Survey of Current Business*, vol. 56 (July 1976) and vol. 57 (January 1977), tables 1.1 and 2.1 in each.

personal income were much smaller than those of GNP, providing evidence of the operation of the automatic stabilizers.

Although the automatic stabilizers act to prevent sharp upward and downward movements of GNP, they do not ensure full-employment GNP. If the economy were at full employment and something brought about a decrease in planned private spending, the automatic fiscal stabilizers would reduce the impact of the fall in spending on GNP but they would not reverse it. Discretionary action would be required to restore full-employment GNP unless something else happened to restore private spending.

Other Limitations of Fiscal Policy

As mentioned earlier, fiscal actions that cause budget deficits or surpluses tend to generate monetary counterforces that may reduce or increase the stimulatory or restrictive effect of the initial policy. Consider, for example, the case where GNP rises because government expenditures are increased or taxes are cut. If the rise in GNP is not accompanied by an increase in the supply of money or other liquid assets, individuals and firms will have fewer liquid assets relative to their incomes than they had before. It is generally believed that individuals and firms will accept an illiquid position only at high interest rates or yields. If higher interest rates are required to induce the private sector to accept a poorer liquidity position, at least part of the expansive effect of increased government purchases or lower taxes will be offset by these higher rates. Private spending, particularly for residential construction and business investment in plant and equipment, is to some degree sensitive to interest rates. Businessmen will forgo projects when the cost of borrowing approaches or exceeds the return on a project. Therefore, higher interest rates brought about by the efforts of firms and individuals to reach an acceptable liquidity position will have some restraining effect on private spending, thus offsetting in part the expansive effect of fiscal policy. In short, financing government deficits by issuing debt may crowd out private borrowers, with most of the effect falling on investment.[6] Reduction in consumer and business spending will reduce the initial multiplier effect of the fiscal stimulus.

6. This point is discussed further in chapter 7.

The Appropriate Budget Policy

When discretionary fiscal policy is used, one important consideration must be taken into account in deciding on the proper mix of
changes in tax rates and expenditures—government expenditures
and taxes play fundamentally different roles in the economy. When
the government decides to spend money, it is allocating resources
between the public and private sectors. In cutting taxes, it increases
individuals' command over resources and increases the private use of
resources. This being so, it would seem that the allocation function
of government expenditures should not be distorted by their use for
fiscal policy reasons. Expenditures should ideally be set at that level
which achieves the public's desired allocation of resources between
the public and the private sector. If the public wants one-fifth of full-
employment output to go to defense and other federal activities,
expenditures should be set to produce this result. Or if it would rather
have more automobiles and recreation, public expenditures should be
adjusted accordingly. Then, given the level of public expenditures
that the people prefer, tax rates and transfers should be adjusted to
produce the level of planned spending needed to promote or maintain
full employment and price stability.

However, tax rate changes are not a perfect weapon for affecting
planned spending. If frequently used, they may disrupt business planning and result in a deterioration of the tax system. Furthermore, as
already noted, it may be difficult to gain quick approval for a tax
change, even though such a change might be the best means of
achieving the fiscal policy goal. Finally, if changes in tax rates are
perceived to be only temporary, they may be of only limited effectiveness: a temporary tax increase, for example, may simply result
in reduced savings, with no significant effect on consumption expenditures. Similarly, a temporary tax cut to stimulate the economy may
be dissipated by increased savings, with no increase in consumers'
spending. Because of these constraints, discretionary fiscal policy
relies on changes in government spending in addition to tax rate
changes.

What are the implications of this for budget balance? They clearly
depend on the state of the economy and on private spending pro-
pensities. If private spending is increasing sharply, tax rates will
have to be raised or government spending cut to prevent inflation.

This combination of circumstances will tend to produce a budget surplus. On the other hand, if private spending is weak, tax rates may have to be adjusted downward or expenditures upward (or both) to restore full employment. This policy will lead to a budget deficit.

It seems obvious that a budget surplus or deficit is not an end in itself; the objective is to maintain stable growth. Persistent deficits may be necessary to achieve full employment, or it may be possible to achieve full employment with a balanced budget or with a surplus. If fiscal policy is used properly, alone or in conjunction with monetary policy, surpluses or deficits will occur. Whether discretionary fiscal policy should rely more heavily on tax-transfer changes or on changes in expenditures is a matter not only of efficiency and feasibility, but also of political ideology.

Those who emphasize variations in tax rates rather than in expenditure levels base their argument on two propositions: expenditures should be set at a level reflecting the citizens' preferences about the allocation of goods between the public and private sectors; and enlarging the public sector reduces the choices for the private sector. Others believe that setting a level of government expenditures without regard to its stabilization role is neither feasible nor prudent. Since expenditure changes are more potent weapons than tax changes, they believe that public spending, specifically on public works projects, is a useful instrument of fiscal policy. Thus, according to this view, fiscal policy tools should not be restricted to manipulating taxes and transfers.

Public works projects typically involve construction of schools, government offices, sewer systems, and similar projects usually undertaken by private businesses on government contracts. These projects have several features that make them at least potentially attractive and effective instruments of fiscal policy. Construction or repair of many capital projects (though not necessarily schools) can, for example, be postponed when the economy is expanding so that, when a recession occurs, there will be a backlog of such projects available to stimulate employment. Furthermore, these projects can, in principle (once again excepting schools), be aimed at those areas of the country where unemployment is most severe.

The disadvantages of public works projects also need to be considered. Perhaps the chief among these relates to the timing of the projects. For one thing, construction projects frequently take a long

Table 6-1. New Obligational Authority, Obligations, and Expenditures under the Public Works Acceleration Program, Fiscal Years 1963-70
Millions of dollars

| | New obligational authority | Obligations | | | |
| | | State and local projects | Federal projects | Adminis-tration | Expenditures |
Fiscal year					
1963	850.0	96.7	55.0	3.0	62.5
1964	30.0	313.7	81.8	1.9	331.8
1965	4.0	192.3	15.7	0.6	321.6
1966	...	...	...	...	88.2
1967	...	...	...	...	21.1
1968	...	...	...	...	5.0
1969	...	...	...	...	2.0
1970	...	...	...	...	0.8
Total	884.0	602.7	152.5	5.5	833.0

Source: Nancy H. Teeters, "The 1972 Budget: Where It Stands and Where It Might Go," *Brookings Papers on Economic Activity, 1:1971*, p. 233.

time to complete, yet once started they must be finished; half a bridge is worthless. Perhaps even more important is the time it takes to get the projects started. As a case in point, consider the accelerated public works program signed into law in 1962.[7] Less than 10 percent of the spending under this program took place during fiscal year 1963; most of the spending occurred in fiscal years 1964 and 1965, and almost 15 percent occurred in later years (see table 6-1).

Regardless of which school of thought one leans to, there are merits and disadvantages to both. Discretionary fiscal policy has in the past and will continue in the future to rely on both tax and expenditure changes to achieve its objectives.

Alternative Budget Proposals

The essence of modern fiscal policy is the idea that the federal government, by varying taxes, expenditures, or both, can offset fluctuations in the level of planned spending and output. As indicated earlier, this policy will result in budget deficits or budget surpluses.

Although countercyclical fiscal policy has been used by all presidents since the early 1960s and has been endorsed by business and

7. Public Works Acceleration Act, September 14, 1962 (P.L. 87-658).

labor groups and by expert bodies such as the Commission on Money and Credit, it has not been fully accepted by the general public. Whenever discretionary fiscal policy results in budget deficits, budget policy is termed "fiscally irresponsible" and the call for balancing the budget is made. The belief that the government should "balance" its budget has "run the gamut from naive diatribes about the evils of deficit spending to the more sophisticated work of the Committee for Economic Development and sometimes the Council of Economic Advisers."[8] Proposals for balancing the budget have been made by various groups. The most widely known of these in this country are the "stabilizing budget" proposal of the Committee for Economic Development and the "Swedish budget policy."

The Stabilizing Budget Proposals

The CED proposal—the "stabilizing budget"—suggests setting federal government purchases of goods and services at a "needs" level, fixing tax rates so that a "moderate surplus" would be generated at a "high employment" level of GNP,[9] and then letting the automatic fiscal stabilizers work to even out the periods of prosperity and recession in the economy.

The CED sees several virtues in the program. First, it would stabilize the economy; as was noted in our discussion of automatic fiscal stabilizers (see figure 6-1), fiscal stabilizers have been effective in the postwar period. Second, it would provide at least some of the budget discipline of the annually balanced budget; every new expenditure would require higher tax rates to maintain the planned surplus at high employment.[10] Finally, it would permit some retirement of the public debt, presuming that the economy would tend to fluctuate around the high-employment level of GNP and that the surpluses in good years would be cumulatively greater than the deficits in bad years.

8. Blinder and Solow, "Analytical Foundations," p. 37.

9. See the committee's publications, *Taxes and the Budget: A Program for Prosperity in a Free Economy* (CED, 1947) and *Fiscal and Monetary Policy for High Employment* (CED, 1961).

10. Actually, the CED proposal allows for changes in government spending unmatched by tax rate changes (1) where the surplus at high employment (defined as 96 percent by the CED) is growing because GNP is growing as the result of increases in the labor force and its productivity, (2) where there is an urgent need for an extraordinary expenditure of a temporary nature, and (3) in the event of a severe economic depression or major inflation.

Similar proposals have been made by Milton Friedman and Gunnar Myrdal.[11] The Friedman proposal differs from the CED proposal mainly in proposing that the budget be balanced at high employment and that federal deficits and surpluses be financed by issuing money or retiring interest-bearing government securities. The Myrdal proposal, known as the "Swedish budget," differs mainly in that it provides for a cyclically balanced budget rather than a modest surplus over the cycle.

The automatic stabilizing budget programs are open to several criticisms. First, although they allow the automatic stabilizers to stabilize the economy, they do not necessarily stabilize it around the desired level. Given government spending, as determined on a "needs" basis and the appropriate monetary policy, only one level of tax rates in a particular period of time will generate full employment and this level of tax rates (together with the planned amount of government expenditures) may result in a surplus, in a balanced budget, or in a deficit at high (or full) employment. Achieving the goal of a moderate surplus or a balanced budget at full employment may thus not be possible at all times. Where full employment and stable prices can be achieved only with a planned deficit, a surplus or a balanced budget will only frustrate the objective. Where they are consistent only with a large budget surplus, setting tax rates to produce a balanced budget, or too small a surplus, will tend to raise prices. In short, there can be no rigidly fixed rule for the proper surplus or deficit at full-employment GNP when the economy has more than one goal and only one type of fiscal policy.

A second difficulty with this kind of budget program arises from changes in the world situation or domestic crises that may call for substantial and frequent changes in government purchases of goods and services. Such unpredictable events as the Korean War, the launching of Sputnik, the Berlin and Cuban crises, or the Vietnam conflict may cause sharp changes in federal spending. Under the stabilizing budget proposals, each unexpected change would call for

11. Friedman, "A Monetary and Fiscal Framework for Economic Stability," *American Economic Review*, vol. 38 (June 1948), pp. 245–64, reprinted in his *Essays in Positive Economics* (University of Chicago Press, 1953), pp. 133–56; and Myrdal, "Fiscal Policy in the Business Cycle," *American Economic Review*, vol. 29 (March 1939, pt. 2 [Supplement], *Papers and Proceedings, 1938*), pp. 183–93, reprinted in Arthur Smithies and J. Keith Butters, eds., *Readings in Fiscal Policy* (Irwin for the American Economic Association, 1955), pp. 67–79.

corresponding changes in tax rates to maintain the planned surplus at high employment.[12] Aside from the impracticability of trying to secure such tax changes from Congress every time a change in expenditures is required, the initial effect of increases in government spending and taxes at full-employment GNP would not be neutral in its effect on the budget balance. Even without emergency changes, there would be a slow and probably continuous rise in government expenditures as a result of normal population growth and the resulting demands for government services. If tax rates were raised correspondingly, the initial effect again would not be neutral.[13] As government expenditures rose, the budget surplus at full-employment GNP would have to rise correspondingly to keep the same fiscal impact. The rule prescribing a response to the budget surplus at full-employment GNP would therefore have to be continually revised, which makes the automatic budget considerably less automatic and much more discretionary.

Formula Flexibility

Another suggestion for an automatic budget policy is "formula flexibility." Under a formula system, tax rate changes (and perhaps government expenditure changes) are legislated in advance, so that they will occur automatically when changes in certain indexes of business activity occur. For example, legislation might provide for an automatic tax cut if real GNP should fall by a certain percentage or an automatic tax increase tied to a certain percentage rise. Such provisions would operate like the automatic fiscal stabilizers.

This plan has much that is appealing. It would avoid congressional delay in using tax rate changes as a stabilizing device and would add considerable potency to the fiscal arsenal. The new congressional budget process offers policymakers the opportunity for implementing some form of formula flexibility. In formulating the first concurrent resolution, the budget committee could recommend tax or expenditure changes that would go into effect when GNP falls or rises by certain amounts. That is, if current forecasts seem to indicate a fall in the

12. Although the CED budget proposal allows for extraordinary changes in federal spending without tax rate changes, it specifies that these should be temporary changes and in addition implies that they should not occur often. But they do occur often and in many cases are not temporary.

13. The long-run effects might be neutral if the effects of budget surpluses or deficits on private spending were considered.

rate of growth of GNP, a certain tax reduction or an expenditure increase (over and above that requested in the President's budget) could be incorporated in the budget resolution and approved on a contingent basis by appropriate legislation, to become effective as primary data confirming the forecast become available.

Summary

Expenditures and receipts of the federal government, by virtue of their magnitude, have considerable impact on the economy. If they were to be programmed without an awareness of their overall impact, the effects, such as extensive unemployment or serious inflationary pressure, could be disastrous.

Modern fiscal policy relies on discretionary changes in the level of government purchases of goods and services and tax rates (given the proper monetary policy) to produce full-employment GNP with stable prices without regard to the resulting budget deficit or surplus, and allows the automatic fiscal stabilizers to reduce the amplitude of periodic swings of GNP around the full-employment level.

Proposals have also been designed for an automatic stabilizing budget: to fix a goal of a certain budget surplus or deficit at full-employment output and let the automatic stabilizers work. These were shown to meet the objectives of fiscal discipline but unfortunately they impose rigid rules that do not necessarily represent the best response in many economic situations.

CHAPTER SEVEN

Fiscal Policy
and the National Debt

THE FEDERAL GOVERNMENT may incur budget deficits for two reasons: to stabilize the economy by increasing the level of total demand for goods and services in periods of unemployment and weak private demand; or because spending in periods of high employment exceeds tax receipts. In this latter case, the federal deficit is independent of the stabilization role usually associated with budget deficits.

A look at the federal budget trends shown in figure 4-6 reveals that over the last few years the federal government has been running increasing deficits. The outlook seems, at least for the short run, to be one of additional deficits. This means that the size of the national debt will continue to rise in the next few years with little assurance that a budget balance will be restored at full employment.

It is precisely this possibility that disturbs many critics of compensatory fiscal policy. In their view a growing budget deficit increases the size of government relative to the private sector, "crowds out" private investors by withdrawing from the capital market funds that would otherwise have been used to increase private capital formation, aggravates inflationary tendencies and threatens the nation's stability.[1] In addition, critics of budget deficits argue that increases in the national debt "impose a burden on future generations."

The "crowding out" argument was emphasized in statements by both the secretary of the treasury and the chairman of the Federal Reserve System. Chairman Arthur Burns testified that if the federal government were to run too large a deficit, "enormous strains . . . may be placed on money and capital markets. This means that interest rates may begin to shoot up, that many private borrowers may be crowded out of the market, that savings funds may once more be diverted from mortgage lenders, and that the stock market may turn weak again."[2]

Secretary William Simon, calling the 1976 budget deficits dangerous, stated that "excessive Federal demands on the capital markets would set in motion a vicious competition between the government and private borrowers for capital funds. Inevitably, mortgage borrowers . . . would be crowded out of the marketplace."[3] In contrast to these views was the statement of Arthur Okun, former chairman of the President's Council of Economic Advisers: "Of all the national economic problems facing us today, the one that is most exaggerated is that of financing the deficit. . . . We face a huge federal deficit because private saving is outrunning private investment by a wide margin. And that generates a superfluity of credit supplies relative to private credit demands which will absorb short-term Treasury securities very happily."[4]

In addition to the "crowding out" issue, both economists and policymakers have also voiced concern for future generations, as in a statement such as the following:

One of the greatest crimes of all . . . is one that is rarely considered by many Americans to be an offense at all. . . .

The full effects of this crime will not likely fall upon the generation that

1. See "Minority Views of James L. Buckley and James A. McClure," in *First Concurrent Resolution on the Budget—Fiscal Year 1976,* Report of the Senate Committee on the Budget, Report 94-77 (GPO, 1975), pp. 135–50.

2. Chairman Arthur F. Burns's testimony on March 13, 1975, before the Senate Committee on the Budget, reprinted in ibid., p. 29.

3. Testimony of William E. Simon in *The 1976 First Concurrent Resolution on the Budget,* Hearings before the Senate Committee on the Budget, 94:1 (GPO, 1975), vol. 2, pp. 1030–31.

4. Arthur M. Okun, "What's Wrong with the U.S. Economy? Diagnosis and Prescription," *Quarterly Review of Economics and Business,* vol. 15 (Summer 1975), p. 30 (Brookings General Series Reprint 305).

is committing it, but may call for reckoning far in the future, and, unless the present trend is reversed, each succeeding generation will pay more heavily for it. The offense is being compounded annually, and its long-range effects are cause for serious alarm. This is the crime: the generation that controls the economy of this nation today and those who have important government responsibility are callously and mercilessly burdening the livelihood and earnings of the generations that will follow us with a tremendous oppressive national debt.

 . . . We are saddling our grandchildren . . . with the bills for our luxurious living. We have no moral right to do this.[5]

Others, however, argue that such a concern is unfounded; that the national debt imposes no burden since we "owe it to ourselves"; that "the real issue . . . [is] whether it is possible by internal borrowing to shift a real burden from the present generation, in the sense of the present economy as a whole, onto a future generation, in the sense of the future economy as a whole. What is important for economists is to teach . . . that the latter is impossible because a project that uses up resources needs the resources at the time that it uses them up, and not before or after."[6]

These conflicting views concerning the size of the federal budget deficits and the national debt raise the following questions: Who is right? Is there a real danger to the private economy from large and continued budget deficits? Is there a burden imposed by a national debt? Does the national debt lead to inflation and government bankruptcy? These questions are obviously crucial to the design of a fiscal program.

First, a definition of "national debt" is called for. Next is a brief summary of data relating the growth of the national debt to other economic magnitudes. The remainder of the chapter deals with the issues surrounding the national debt: (1) the burden of the debt in a deficit setting that has come about through attempts to alleviate unemployment by use of increased expenditures or reduced taxes; (2) the burden of the debt in a full-employment setting; and (3) other issues connected with the debt, such as inflation and national solvency.[7]

5. Senator John L. McClellan, "The Crime of National Insolvency," *Tax Review*, vol. 24 (January 1963), pp. 2–3.

6. Abba P. Lerner, "The Burden of Debt," in James M. Ferguson, ed., *Public Debt and Future Generations* (University of North Carolina Press, 1964), p. 93.

7. To simplify the discussion of the issues, it will be assumed that all federal debt

Table 7-1. Federal Debt, by Type of Security, June 30, 1976

Type of security	Billions of dollars
Interest-bearing public issues	489.5
Marketable	392.6
Treasury bills, certificates, and notes	353.0
Treasury bonds	39.6
Nonmarketable	94.6
U.S. savings bonds and notes	70.1
Foreign[a]	21.5
Other[b]	3.0
Convertible bonds	2.3
Special issues	129.8
Total gross federal debt[c]	620.4

Source: *Federal Reserve Bulletin*, vol. 62 (July 1976), p. A34.

a. Certificates of indebtedness, notes, and bonds in the Treasury foreign series and foreign-currency-series issues.

b. Depository, retirement plan, state and local government, and Rural Electrification Administration bonds and Treasury deposit funds.

c. Includes noninterest-bearing debt (of which $613 million on June 30, 1976, was not subject to statutory debt limitation).

Definition of the National Debt

The federal debt consists of direct obligations or debts of the U.S. Treasury and obligations of federal government enterprises or agencies. In table 7-1 the debt is broken down into "public issues"—that part of total debt held by private investors and the Federal Reserve System—and "special issues," that part held only by government agencies and trust funds. Of the issues sold to the public, some are "marketable"—that is, they are traded on securities markets—and some are "nonmarketable" and cannot be traded (for example, U.S. savings bonds). The latter may, however, be redeemed in cash or converted into another issue.

Distribution of the debt by types of holders as of June 1976 is shown in table 7-2. Of the total, about 40 percent was held by government agencies, trust funds, and the Federal Reserve banks. Trust fund holdings are largely in the form of special issues, while those of the Federal Reserve are of the marketable type and are acquired through its open market operations. Of privately held debt, 26 percent was held by individuals, mostly in the form of savings bonds, another 26 percent by commercial and mutual savings banks, 19 per-

is held by residents of the United States. This is not far from the truth: in 1976 about 89 percent of federal debt was held domestically.

Table 7-2. Ownership of Federal Debt, by Type of Holder, June 30, 1976
Par value

Type of holder	Billions of dollars
U.S. government agencies and trust funds	149.6
Federal Reserve banks	94.4
Private investors	376.4
Domestic	306.5
Individuals	96.4
Commercial and mutual savings banks	96.9
State and local governments	39.5
Other	73.7
Foreign and international	69.8
Total gross federal debt	620.4

Source: *Federal Reserve Bulletin*, vol. 62 (December 1976), p. A34. Figures are rounded.

cent by foreign and international investors, and the remaining 29 percent by state and local governments and other private investors.

Almost all federal debt is issued by the Treasury Department. However, a few federal agencies are authorized to issue debt of their own, which is sold directly to the public or to other government agencies and funds. At the beginning of fiscal year 1977, the outstanding debt issued by these agencies was $11.7 billion.[8] As a result of the creation of the Federal Financing Bank, which buys new issues of agency debt and finances its purchases by borrowing from the Treasury, agency debt is expected to decline in the future. To prevent double counting, these holdings are excluded from gross federal debt.

The relationship between the budget deficit and the change in the size of the debt is shown in table 7-3. As the table indicates, the unified budget deficit or surplus is the principal determinant of the change in the federal debt. However, the unified budget deficit or surplus, together with off-budget federal agencies' deficit or surplus, is a better indication of the change in the size of the debt held by the public.[9]

Statutory limitations have been placed on the amount of the federal debt (debt ceiling). The debt subject to the limit includes virtually all Treasury debt but excludes the major part of debt issued directly to the public by federal agencies (which is subject to special statutory limits). Although the ceiling on the amount of national debt out-

8. *The Budget of the United States Government, Fiscal Year 1978*, p. 208.
9. Among off-budget federal entities are the rural electrification and telephone revolving fund, Rural Telephone Bank, housing for the elderly or handicapped fund, Pension Benefit Guaranty Corporation, and the Postal Service fund.

Table 7-3. Budget Financing and Change in Gross Federal Debt, Fiscal Year 1976

Description	Billions of dollars
Federal funds, deficit	68.9
Transactions with the public[a]	40.6
Transactions with trust funds	28.2
Minus: Trust funds, surplus	2.4
Transactions with the public	−25.8
Transactions with federal funds	28.2
Unified budget deficit	66.5
Plus: Off-budget federal agencies, deficit	7.2
Total deficit	**73.7**
Plus: Change in means of financing other than borrowing from the public[b]	9.3
Total requirements for borrowing from the public	82.9
Plus: Reclassification of securities	0.5
Change in debt held by the public	83.4
Plus: Change in federal agency investments in federal debt	4.3
Change in gross federal debt	**87.7**

Source: *The Budget of the United States Government, Fiscal Year 1978*, pp. 206, 210. Figures are rounded.

a. Payments from federal funds to the general revenue sharing trust fund are treated as transactions with the public instead of transactions with a trust fund. The corresponding payments from the general revenue sharing trust fund are omitted.

b. This includes change in cash and monetary assets, change in liabilities for checks outstanding, change in deposit fund balances, and seigniorage on coins.

standing has been imposed by Congress since 1917, it has almost always been adjusted upward to accommodate Treasury borrowing to finance government operations. The ceiling on the debt subject to limit was set at $700 billion through September 30, 1977, when it was scheduled to return to the permanent limit of $400 billion. Under the congressional budget act of 1974, a new procedure for determining the limit was instituted. Congress is to include in its concurrent resolutions on the budget the appropriate level of the federal debt and the amount by which the debt subject to the limit should be increased. The first concurrent resolution on the budget adopted by Congress May 17, 1977, recommended a public debt for fiscal year 1977 of $708 billion. To permit the federal government to meet its obligations, the ceiling will have to be raised again as long as deficits are incurred.

Gross and Net Federal Debt

In discussing the federal debt, the concept of gross federal debt or national debt has been used. Gross federal debt includes the federal government borrowing from the public, government agencies' bor-

Table 7-4. Gross and Net Federal Debt, Selected Years, 1915–76ᵃ
Billions of dollars

End of calendar year	Federal debt		End of calendar year	Federal debt	
	Gross	*Net*		*Gross*	*Net*
1915	1.2	1.2	1950	256.7	199.9
1919	25.8	25.3	1960	290.2	210.0
1930	16.0	14.9	1966	329.3	219.2
1933	23.8	21.4	1970	389.2	229.9
1940	50.9	41.2	1971	424.1	247.9
1942	112.5	94.1	1972	449.3	262.5
1943	170.1	141.6	1973	469.9	261.7
1944	232.1	191.7	1974ᵇ	492.7	271.0
1945	278.7	227.4	1975ᵇ	576.6	349.4
1946	259.1	208.3	1976ᵇ	653.5	409.5ᶜ

Sources: Raymond W. Goldsmith, *A Study of Saving in the United States*, vol. 1 (Princeton University Press, 1955), pp. 535, 985; Board of Governors of the Federal Reserve System, *Banking and Monetary Statistics* (FRB, 1943), p. 509; FRB, *Banking and Monetary Statistics, 1941–1970* (FRB, 1976), p. 882; *Economic Report of the President, January 1976*, p. 254; *Treasury Bulletin* (February 1977), pp. 21, 67. Net debt for 1930 and 1933 are averages of June data for the respective year and the following year, from **FRB**, *Banking and Monetary Statistics* (1943), p. 512.

a. Gross federal debt is federal government borrowing from the public plus government agencies' borrowing plus debt holdings of the Federal Reserve System; net federal debt is federal government borrowing from the public.

b. Beginning July 1974, excludes noninterest-bearing notes issued to the International Monetary Fund, to conform with presentations in the budget documents.

c. Preliminary.

rowings, and debt holdings of the Federal Reserve System. A more useful concept is that of the net federal debt held by the public. Net federal debt is defined as gross federal debt less the holdings of the Federal Reserve System and government investment accounts. This concept, rather than that of the gross federal debt, is the relevant one to use in analyzing the impact of the federal debt on the economy because it reflects the public's ability and willingness to absorb government securities in place of private securities. At the end of 1976, gross federal debt amounted to $654 billion while net federal debt was $410 billion, or about 60 percent of the gross debt. Table 7-4 shows the growth of gross and net federal debt for selected years during the period 1915–76.

The principal causes of the growth of the federal debt have been wars and depressions. During World War I the federal debt rose sharply from about $1 billion in 1915 to a level of almost $26 billion by the end of 1919. From there it decreased about $10 billion to $16 billion in 1930. The economic depression of the 1930s led to government deficit spending, and the federal debt increased by approximately $35 billion between 1930 and 1940. During World War II it grew tremendously, reaching $259 billion in December 1946. Since 1946 the debt has continued to grow, especially during years of recession. From 1965 to 1975, the gross federal debt increased almost 100 percent, a considerably larger increase than occurred from the mid-forties to the mid-sixties (it rose by only 37 percent from 1944 to 1964).

The fact that most of the growth of the debt occurred during major wars does not in itself mean that debt inevitably accompanies war. During recessions and periods of weak planned spending, expansionary fiscal policy is called for to promote economic recovery. Increasing government spending or cutting taxes, or both, produce federal deficits and an increase in the size of the federal debt. Over the period 1914–75, out of accumulated budget deficits of $447.4 billion, 60 percent was incurred during war years and about 21 percent during recession years.

Data on the Federal Debt

Looking at the growth of the gross or net federal debt in isolation reveals little except that it has grown tremendously over the years the U.S. government has been in existence. Gross federal debt rose from $1 billion in 1915 to $654 billion in 1976 and net federal debt rose to $410 billion during the period. But many other economic measures have risen spectacularly, in particular the volume of output and private debt. Likewise, federal net interest payments have grown immensely over the years, but so has our ability to carry them.

To get some perspective on the growth of federal debt, it is useful to make the comparisons shown in figures 7-1 to 7-3. Figure 7-1 shows, for five-year intervals from 1900 to 1930 and annually thereafter, the net federal debt and the ratio of the net federal debt to GNP (in current dollars). The debt–GNP ratio was very low up to 1916, rose sharply during World War I, and then declined through the 1920s. In the 1930s it began another rise, which continued through World War II. It has since fallen, and by the 1970s was back almost to the levels that prevailed in the middle 1920s—about 20 percent. In figure 7-2 the growth of gross federal debt is compared with the growth of nonfederal debt since 1900. The figure shows clearly that gross federal debt grew faster than nonfederal debt during the periods

Figure 7-1. Net Federal Debt and Debt as a Percentage of Gross National Product, Five-Year Intervals, 1900–30, and Annually, 1931–76

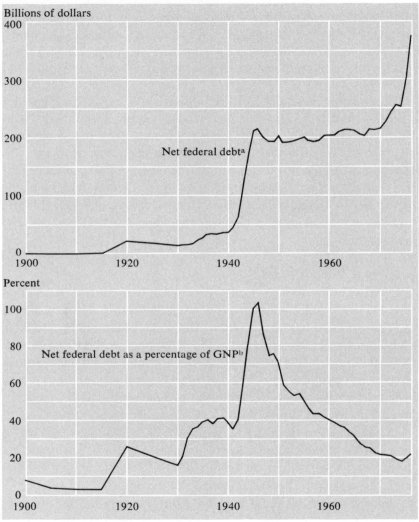

Sources: Debt, 1900–15, and GNP, 1900–25, Raymond W. Goldsmith, *A Study of Saving in the United States,* vol. 1 (Princeton University Press, 1955), pp. 535, 985, and Goldsmith and others, *A Study of Saving in the United States,* vol. 3 (Princeton University Press, 1956), p. 427; debt, 1920–39, derived from Board of Governors of the Federal Reserve System, *Banking and Monetary Statistics* (FRB, 1943), pp. 509–10, 512; debt, 1940–66, FRB, *Banking and Monetary Statistics, 1941–1970* (FRB, 1976), pp. 882–83; debt, 1967–76, *Economic Report of the President, January 1977,* p. 275; GNP, 1930–76, U.S. Bureau of Economic Analysis, *The National Income and Product Accounts of the United States, 1929–74: Statistical Tables* (GPO, 1977), and *Survey of Current Business,* vol. 56 (July 1976) and vol. 57 (January 1977) issues.
    a. Debt as of June 30 of each year.
    b. Debt as of June 30 of each year; GNP for the calendar year.

Figure 7-2. Gross Federal and Nonfederal Debt, 1920–75a

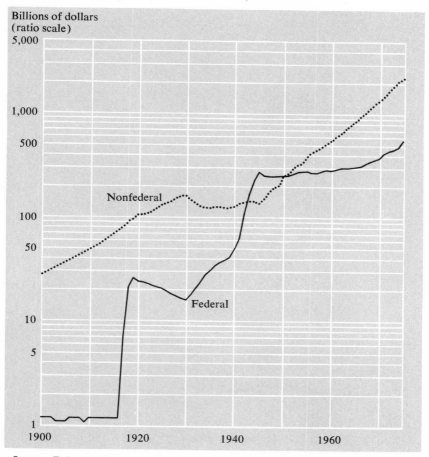

Billions of dollars
(ratio scale)

Sources: Federal debt, same as table 7-4; nonfederal debt, 1900 and 1912, Board of Governors of the Federal Reserve System; other nonfederal debt, appendix table A-9.
a. End-of-year data. State and local government debt is not included in the nonfederal. Because the vertical axes are ratio scale, the steep lines show the rates of growth of federal and private debt.

1917–19 and 1930–45, but that in the other fifty-seven years of the seventy-six-year period, nonfederal debt grew faster.[10]

Finally, figure 7-3 shows net interest paid on the federal debt, both in dollars and as a percentage of GNP. Since 1900, interest paid on the federal debt has not reached 2.0 percent of GNP, a level almost

10. Because the vertical axes in figure 7-2 are calibrated according to a ratio scale, the slopes, or steepness of the lines, show the rates of growth of federal and private debt.

Figure 7-3. Net Interest Paid on Federal Debt at Five-Year Intervals, 1900–30, and Annually, 1931–76

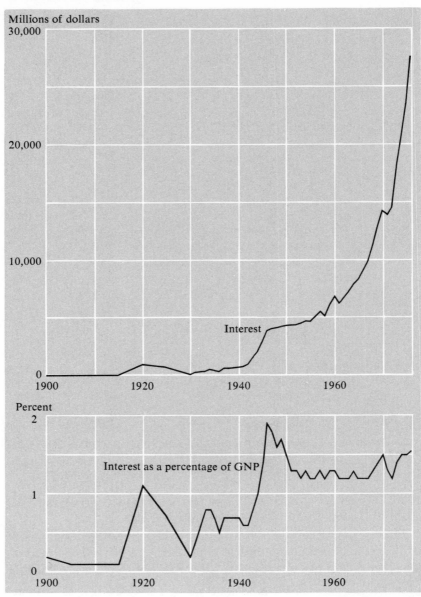

Sources: 1900–25, Goldsmith and others, *Study of Saving,* vol. 3, pp. 427, 445; other years, U.S. Bureau of Economic Analysis, *National Income and Product Accounts of the United States, 1929–74,* and *Survey of Current Business,* July 1976 and January 1977 issues.

reached just after World War II. The percentage fell to 1.2 in 1953 and hovered between 1.2 and 1.3 until the late 1960s, then rose again, reaching 1.6 percent in 1976. The growth of federal debt, then, though large in absolute terms, appears less awesome when it is related to the growth of output or of private debt.

Federal Borrowing and the "Crowding Out" Effect

Since 1901, the federal budget has been in a deficit position for forty-nine years out of seventy-six. Budget deficits, especially in peacetime, have always been a source of alarm to those who represent the "conservative" view on fiscal matters. Defenders of deficit spending were in the past successful in persuading the nation of the wisdom of compensatory fiscal action: they dismissed as groundless the fear connected with large federal deficits during recessions or weak private demand. However, the relatively large size of the budget deficit for 1976, and of those projected for fiscal years 1977 and 1978, revived some of this fear. The "crowding out" effect of deficit spending is now a part of everyday journalistic language whenever the issue of federal deficit or public borrowing is discussed. What is "crowding out"? Crowding out is a term used to describe the adverse effect of government deficit on private investment.

To understand this issue as well as to gain an insight into the validity of some of the statements on "crowding out" made earlier in the chapter requires first an understanding of the relation between the deficit and the debt—the financing aspect of the federal deficit.

When the federal government runs a deficit it can finance it by one or more of the following means: drawing down Treasury cash balances; selling securities to the Federal Reserve System; selling securities to commercial banks; and selling securities to nonbank investors. Regardless of which of these methods is selected, a federal deficit leads to a dollar-for-dollar increase in the net financial assets of nonbank investors (or households).[11] Although all these methods of

11. If the deficit is financed by drawing down Treasury cash balances, the public's money holding will increase by the amount of the deficit. Likewise, if it is financed by selling securities to commercial banks, the banks pay for the securities by creating demand deposits for the Treasury—deposits which, when spent by the government, add to the public's holdings of money and so on. For a detailed discussion on financing the federal deficit, see Council of Economic Advisers Staff Memorandum, "Financing a Federal Deficit," in Warren L. Smith and Ronald L. Teigen, eds., *Readings in Money, National Income, and Stabilization Policy* (3d ed., Irwin, 1974), pp. 323–25.

financing the debt affect private saving, the method chosen will have a different effect on the economy and thus on the effectiveness of the fiscal action for which the deficit was originally created.

There are two effects to consider: the effect of fiscal action producing the deficit, which is always expansionary; and the effect of the method of financing the deficit, which depends to a large extent on the action taken by the Federal Reserve System. As was noted in chapter 5, an expansionary fiscal policy—an increase in government expenditures, a cut in taxes, or both—will increase the aggregate level of demand and output through the multiplier effect. However, the monetary aspect of the deficit—the financing method chosen—will also have an effect on the level of output, prices, and aggregate demand. A deficit policy that increases aggregate demand and output stimulates the demand for money balances. If the Federal Reserve System were not to accommodate fiscal actions by increasing the money supply (by buying government securities), the deficit would be financed by selling debt to the nonbanking public, such as insurance companies, other corporations, state and local governments, and individuals, or to commercial banks. Unless the Federal Reserve increases bank reserves, interest rates will rise and this will have a restraining effect on private spending, partly offsetting the expansionary effect of the deficit. The recent discussions of the "crowding out" of private spending by fiscal action are discussions of precisely this point. Unless the monetary authority is willing to monetize part of the debt, to add to commercial bank reserves, "crowding out" will occur and private spending will decline, thus offsetting part of the stimulus the deficit is supposed to create.

How serious is crowding out? And what is the impact of additional debt on the economy? The next two sections will attempt to answer these questions, first, in a setting where unemployment prevails, and second, in a full-employment setting.

The Burden of the Debt in an Unemployment Setting

Hostility to the size of the national debt as well as to its continued growth generally arises from the view that the debt will reduce private capital formation and impose a burden on future generations. To decide whether this view is justified, we will first consider a society where there is unemployment and where the government plans to run a deficit to finance additional expenditures or to cut taxes in order to restore output to a full-employment level. The issue then is, does government borrowing to finance a planned deficit create a burden for future generations?

In one sense at least, there is clearly no burden on later generations. A closed society cannot dispose of more goods and services than it currently produces; it cannot borrow tomorrow's output today. In a period of unemployment there is essentially no competition between the government and the private sector for resources. Goods and services acquired by the government at the time of the expenditure do not reduce the output available to consumers or private investors. Deficit financing to restore full employment leaves future generations better off to the extent that private investment is stimulated, inasmuch as in the absence of an expenditure increase or tax cut, the added investment would probably not take place and future generations would have a smaller stock of private capital and lower output. A further gain in future output (and thus a gain to future generations) results from government spending of an investment type—as, for example, for schools, bridges, and roads.

What about the interest payments on the debt and the possible repayment of the principal that falls to the lot of future generations; are these not a burden? The answer is a qualified no. There is no aggregate burden on future generations that must make interest payments on the debt and perhaps repay the principal, for these are simply *transfers* of income (or wealth) among members of society. There may be "distributional effects"—wealth may be redistributed from taxpayers to bondholders to the extent that these are not the same individuals—but these do not necessarily leave the community in worse circumstances in the aggregate. However, the debt still imposes some burden on future generations because future taxes must be levied to service the debt. To illustrate this point, suppose that an individual exchanges his holdings of a government bond for a private bond with equal yield (discounting risk differential). At the time of the purchase the position of the individual would be the same. But what about future periods? With the public bond, the taxpayer is subjected to an "involuntary" levy in order to finance the interest payments on the debt, while no such levy would exist in the case of the private bond. This is the "real" cost of debt-financed public spending; public projects financed by debt creation do not explicitly yield revenues to meet interest payments. No real cost would exist, however, if it could be shown that the debt-financed expenditure augments private income sufficiently to offset the tax increase needed to service the debt.[12]

What about "crowding out" of private investors? In an unemployment setting, private demand (consumption and investment) is weak and therefore the demand for funds is likely to fall short of the money available for borrowers. Here Okun's comment cited at the beginning of this chapter would hold; when saving outruns investment demand, suppliers of credit are only too happy to accommodate public borrowing. This was the case in 1975 and 1976 when large federal deficits were accommodated without straining the capital market.

In short, to the extent that public borrowings do not displace private needs, deficit financing and increases in the national debt do not impose a burden on future generations. In fact, running deficits to promote full employment leaves future generations better off in increased real output and investment. In this setting at least, intergenerational equity is not violated.[13]

12. See James M. Buchanan and Richard E. Wagner, *Public Debt in a Democratic Society* (American Enterprise Institute for Public Policy Research, 1967).

13. Franco Modigliani has come to a somewhat different conclusion on this question. He reasons that under certain conditions a deficit created to boost the economy from a depression or recession can leave future generations in circumstances worse than if no government action had been taken. Suppose recessions or depressions are temporary—that is, that the economy will recover eventually even if no government action is taken. Suppose further that consumers and firms together have a plan of desired capital accumulation. A recession then will reduce the present generation's capital below the desired level, since saving and investment are reduced as income falls. The reduction in capital below the desired level will force the members of the present generation to cut their consumption over their lifetimes (even after full employment is restored) to an extent equal to the loss in capital accumulation during the period of unemployment. In short, they will have to save more to accumulate the capital "lost" during the recession. The higher rate of capital formation after full employment is restored will tend, by the time the recession generation dies out, to build the stock of capital back to the level that could have been expected if there had been no temporary unemployment. On the other hand, if the government acts to combat the recession and creates new debt in doing so, the new debt to some extent will replace the "lost" capital in the net worth of investors. Thus the present generation will not seek to build the capital stock back to the planned level; it will be content with government bonds rather than physical capital. Later generations may thus have less private capital than if the government had not attacked the recession by running a deficit.

Of course, the crux of Modigliani's argument is his assumption that recessions are in fact temporary and that government debt is unproductive. If, however, budget deficits are financed by issuing money, and if asset holders receive a stream of real returns from holding money, or if money is a "factor of production," then even in

The Burden of the Debt in a Full-Employment Setting

Now consider a society that is always at full employment regardless of what the government does or does not do about spending, taxes, and the like. Assume that the government plans to spend an additional $10 billion. Will it make any difference if that expenditure is debt-financed or tax-financed?

Because there is full employment, goods and services acquired by the government must always be paid for by a reduction in the output available to the private sector at the time of the expenditure. So, whether tax-financed or debt-financed, the expenditure is immediate; it cannot possibly be paid for by future generations, and thus there is no burden on them in this sense.

As far as interest payments on the debt and possibly repayment of the principal are concerned, here, too, as in the unemployment setting, some burden will be imposed on future generations. However, while it is true that a closed, full-employment community cannot increase today's output by borrowing tomorrow's, the way in which today's output is used can affect the output of tomorrow, and debt financing has an impact on the use of today's output different from that of tax financing or the creation of money. It is through this impact that debt financing of expenditures may impose a significant burden on future generations.

If the economy is at full employment, then by definition the increase in government spending cannot increase total output. Prices will rise whether the increase in government spending is debt-financed, tax-financed, or financed through money creation.[14] But how is investment affected? Suppose an increase in government spending of $10 billion is debt-financed. Taxes on current private income, and therefore private disposable (after-tax) income, will be unchanged. If it is assumed that private consumption depends only

---

Modigliani's argument, debt financing need not impose a burden, whether it occurs in a full-employment or unemployment setting. See his article, "Long-Run Implications of Alternative Fiscal Policies and the Burden of the National Debt," *Economic Journal,* vol. 71 (December 1961), pp. 731–55. For additional discussion of the burden of the debt from the point of view stressing the supply of capital, see Peter A. Diamond, "National Debt in a Neoclassical Growth Model," *American Economic Review,* vol. 55 (December 1965), esp. p. 1141.

14. As noted in chapter 5, an increase in government spending has a larger multiplier effect than an equal increase in taxes. Thus, when taxes are raised to finance government spending, the net effect is expansionary and prices will rise.

on the level of disposable personal income, private consumption of goods will remain unchanged. Because private consumption outlays will be unaffected (and government expenditures will be increasing), the reduction in the private use of output must come out of private investment. Debt financing of an expenditure will thus result in a fall in private investment by the amount of the increase in government spending.[15]

How does this result compare with the result of tax financing a like amount? In the latter case, some part of the tax increase may come out of private personal income. Private consumption will decline as a result of the reduction in disposable personal income, but not by the total amount, since consumers in the aggregate reduce consumption by a fraction of a decrease in disposable personal income. The balance of the impact will fall on private investment. This means that both private consumption and investment will fall, with the total decline in both being just equal to the total increase in government spending. Furthermore, since individuals lack perfect foresight as to future tax policies, financing the deficits through taxation rather than debt issues would not distort individual choices through time; the cost of public expenditures through time cannot be shifted as may be the case when they are financed by issuing debt.

In periods of full employment, the result of money creation is similar to that of tax finance. At high levels of employment, any creation of additional purchasing power must be inflationary and cause the price level to increase. The results are equivalent to a tax on the holders of cash balances. To the extent that real cash balances affect consumption, inflation through money creation will spread the cost of financing the deficit among consumption activities as well as among investment activities.

A comparison of the three methods of financing government deficits during periods of full employment reveals that, although investment falls in both money-financed and tax-financed cases, it falls farther when the government deficit is debt-financed. Here lies the burden on future generations. The burden can be measured in terms of the loss of potential output that will result from the loss of potential

15. Under different assumptions, debt financing need not lead to a fall in private investment by an amount equal to the increase in government spending. To some extent it may reduce consumer spending rather than investment spending.

private capital. That is, debt financing will reduce private investment more than tax financing the same amount, thereby leaving future generations with less capital equipment for production and restricting them to a lower level of private output than would obtain with tax financing.

A final point to consider is the relative productivity of government spending and private spending. If government expenditures are less productive than, or equally as productive as, private investment, the conclusions about the relative burden still hold. If, however, government investment is more productive, future generations will be better off by the reallocation of capital to the public sector, regardless of whether the expenditure is debt-financed, money-financed, or tax-financed; but they will be relatively less well off with debt financing than with money creation or tax financing.[16]

In summary, deficit financing and increases in the national debt in a full-employment setting do not necessarily impose an absolute burden on future generations. If government expenditures are more productive than private investment, future generations will be better off with debt-financed expenditures than without such expenditures. However, it is also clear that, in this setting, future generations will benefit relatively more from such expenditures if they are financed by increasing taxes rather than by increasing the federal debt.

Deficits and Other Issues

As noted in chapter 6, the mere existence of a budget deficit is not a reliable measure of fiscal policy. A large deficit can result from an

---

16. Some economists, notably E. J. Mishan, dispute the validity of the argument that a greater burden is imposed on future generations by borrowing than by taxing, even in a full-employment setting. Mishan argues that, since taxes reduce present consumption and borrowing reduces private capital for future generations, if one talks about a burden being imposed on future generations by borrowing, there is an equal obligation to consider the burden imposed on the present generation by taxing. Every decision society undertakes today affects future generations. Thus decisions to debt-finance government expenditures are no more of a burden on future generations than are decisions by individuals to consume rather than to invest. "After all, we could enormously increase provision for the future if we performed heroic feats of austerity during our lifetimes. Are we then not imposing a heavy burden on these future generations to the extent that we eschew these heroic feats of austerity and instead follow the path of our wonted self-indulgence?" "How To Make a Burden of the Public Debt," *Journal of Political Economy*, vol. 71 (December 1963), p. 540.

anti-inflationary fiscal policy if the government tightens up too much and induces a recession—or if expenditures drop in the private sector and the economy goes into a recession—and federal tax receipts fall as GNP declines. Large deficits occurred in the 1940s during a period of full employment and upward price pressures (which were to some extent suppressed by price and wage controls). On the other hand, during an earlier period, 1931–34, large deficits occurred during a period of severe unemployment and falling prices, and from 1972 to 1976, large deficits occurred with high inflation rates and rising unemployment. Thus there is no real basis for using the actual deficit or surplus to measure the inflationary or deflationary impact of federal fiscal action.

It is often implied that inflation is caused by increasing federal outlays, or that private and state and local government outlays are not inflationary but that federal government outlays are. It is said, too, that private or state and local government outlays are productive whereas federal government outlays are unproductive. GNP is said to be an inaccurate measure of a nation's output, because it includes in total output these unproductive government purchases of goods and services.

Such arguments show a faulty understanding of what determines a nation's output, the nature of output, and the causes of inflation or recession. If government purchases of goods and services are totally unproductive, society might just as well discontinue such outlays and use the resources thus freed in the private sector. It could eliminate expenditures on defense, courts, police, highways, and education, and use the resources to produce more cars, electric shavers, houses, and private planes. It should be obvious that federal (as well as state and local) government expenditures *are* productive in the sense that they satisfy certain social needs that are not met by the private market. These social needs are determined by elected representatives, who are generally (and in theory) responsible to the electorate.

It should be clear also that increases in private outlays for consumption and investment can at times be responsible for inflationary pressures, as they were in 1946–48, 1967–69, and 1973. Whenever excessive aggregate demand is at the root of inflation, the important thing is to bring about a reduction in spending—public and private—through the use of fiscal and monetary actions.

The Public Debt and National Bankruptcy

There is a great deal of emotion in people's attitudes toward the public debt. For example, statements are frequently made to the effect that, if the national debt reaches some particular level, the government's credit standing will be impaired and disaster will follow in the form of something casually referred to as "national bankruptcy." While it is difficult to evaluate these statements, it is not a new idea that there is a limit to the size of the national debt that can be carried without disaster. Individuals have long predicted that a debt of one-tenth, one-fifth, or one-half of the amount we now have would result in national bankruptcy, and they have had to revise the limit upward when it was exceeded and ruin failed to follow.

How much can the federal government borrow? Is there a point beyond which borrowing would have to cease because people would refuse to lend? To answer these questions, one must understand the basis for the credit standing of governments, whether federal, state, or local. Governments have a power not shared by other borrowers; they can impose taxes with which to pay interest on their debt and repay the principal. As long as a government does not abuse its taxing power or extend its credits beyond its capacity to raise taxes, it will have the ability to borrow. It may have to pay high interest charges if its debt becomes large, but it can borrow as long as the public is willing to hold its debt instruments. And this is not all; central governments also have the power to coin and print money. They can always do this, instead of imposing taxes, to meet interest costs on their debts and to transfer resources from the private to the public sector. As a matter of fact, the securities of the U.S. Treasury are looked on by investors as a nearly riskless investment (from the standpoint of possible default on interest payments), despite the enormous increase in the debt in the last half-century.

This does not mean that there is no cause for concern about deficits and the growth of the debt. If the debt is growing because private demand is weak and the government is pursuing a policy of stimulating the economy with tax reductions (or expenditure increases), the deficit is not only harmless but a benefit to the health of the economy. If private spending is strong, however, and prices are rising, low tax rates and a deficit are poor policy indeed. In short, there are good deficits and bad deficits. Good deficits occur when fiscal policy is used to stimulate the economy or to cushion it against economic declines. Bad deficits occur when, in the face of strong private spending, government refuses to raise taxes or reduce expenditures to eliminate inflationary pressures.

The Psychological Effects

It has been held that, even though there may be no danger of burdening future generations, the stimulative effects of increasing the public debt to counteract recessions may be negated or partially offset by public hostility to debt increases. That is, irrational and unwarranted fear of such increases may reduce private spending (particularly investment), thereby offsetting the stimulative effect of the fiscal action producing the deficit. Businessmen may think to themselves, "With such fiscal irresponsibility in the White House, I will not commit my company to new capital outlays."

On the other hand, the announcement of stimulative federal fiscal actions may itself have quite the opposite effect. The stock market's reaction to tax cut suggestions in 1963, 1971, and 1975 and comments in the business press suggest that such positive fiscal action actually encourages business optimism and stimulates investment.

There is no clear answer as to which effect is likely to be dominant. It is hard to single out the effect on businessmen's expectations of any single action of an administration, including the actions of incurring a planned deficit. It is probably true that an administration's overall image has an important psychological influence on business investment decisions, but it is not clear what influence a deficit by itself has or how strong that influence may be.

Summary

From the discussion in this chapter, it is clear that deficits may be economically defensible and even desirable under many conditions. They are undesirable, of course, when the economy is at full employment, when the state of resource allocation is the desired one, and when inflationary pressures exist. If deficits are incurred in an unemployment setting in order to restore full employment, they are all to the good. They tend to increase output and employment and impose no easily identifiable burden on future generations, provided that the use of the idle resources by government is as productive as their use by the private sector. Future interest payments and the repayment of principal are essentially financial transfers involving no aggregate burden. Arguments to the effect that increasing the federal debt will somehow lead to national ruin or bankruptcy have little foundation in fact. And while there may be adverse psychological effects from deficits, there may just as well be salutary ones.

CHAPTER EIGHT

Determining the Level of Federal Spending

THE AMOUNT of federal spending and taxes needed to stabilize the economy has been shown to depend, at least in part, on the state of the economy. When private demand for goods and services is strong, stabilization may call for restraint in expenditures on goods and services, higher tax rates (or a reduction in transfer payments), or both. When private demand is weak, federal taxes may need to be adjusted downward (or transfer payments upward) or expenditures increased, or both.

The role of the federal government in the economy is not, however, limited to stabilization. Even if stabilization goals were satisfied, federal spending would continue to take place to fulfill other important roles in the economy. These roles manifest themselves in the provision of certain goods and services to society at large or for specific individuals. Because of the multiplicity of roles the federal government performs in the economy, there are other grounds for judging the level of federal spending than its total effect on employment, prices, growth, and the balance of payments. Expenditures on nuclear submarines, defense personnel, or defense research, for example, cannot readily be adjusted up or down as private demand weakens or becomes buoyant. Nor can old-age pensions and retirement benefits under social security be juggled to offset ups or downs in private spending, although the timing of payments can be accelerated when necessary. Interest payments on the federal debt and public health are other examples of federal programs that are difficult to vary for countercyclical purposes. While the total amount of spending may be evaluated with an eye to the current state of the economy, and while this evaluation may in turn affect budget decisions on particular programs, the basis for judging individual federal spending programs cannot be solely, or even primarily, their impact on the current level of economic activity.

As was stated in chapter 6, setting the level of federal purchases of goods and services involves choosing between private and public use of resources. Thus, some criterion is needed to guide the policymaker in making such a choice. Decisions concerning the level of transfer payments (the transfer of resources between individuals) or grants-in-aid (the transfer of funds between the federal government and the states and their subdivisions) clearly require criteria different from those needed to determine the level of government expenditures on goods and services. What are these or what should they be?

What criteria can the citizen use, apart from those of stabilization, as a basis for determining whether the overall level of spending or the amounts to be spent on different programs are appropriate? Certainly, citizens have views on these matters, as editorial pages, letters to editors, and casual conversations clearly indicate. They may complain about "wild-eyed spenders" or deplore the neglect of certain federal programs, or both. Yet if they are pressed to explain their views about federal spending proposals in detail, they seldom seem to have objective criteria for judging the need for (or proper level of) federal spending. They may defend a particular program by saying it will "help the community," "create jobs," "meet human needs," or "keep [my] industry prosperous." Or they may attack programs as "unnecessary," "involving a concentration of power in Washington," "better left to the local community," or "profligate and wasteful."

This chapter will investigate criteria for judging federal spending other than stabilization policy, and the extent to which such criteria have been used in determining the level of federal spending.

Purposes of Federal Spending

The basic data for this discussion are presented in table 8-1, where federal expenditures for 1975 are classified according to function and type. Several general features of federal expenditures should be noted. Out of a total of about $358 billion, only $124 billion represents purchases of goods and services. Transfer payments—old age and survivors benefits, and the like—account for $172 billion, and interest paid on the debt amounts to over $23 billion. Another $54 billion represents grants-in-aid to state and local governments.

The expenditure data in table 8-1 are further classified according to whether they use up resources directly—that is, give rise to purchasing power for the federal government—or redistribute resource use between different segments of society. In 1975, the federal government used up $124 billion of resources to meet collective or social needs and transferred about $227 billion to individuals and to state and local governments. Transfer payments to individuals, whether for social security, for unemployment compensation, or to meet interest payments on the federal debt, redistribute purchasing power among individuals without affecting the total level of resources available for private use. On the other hand, transfers to state and local governments (grants-in-aid) may ultimately be used either for state and local government purchases or for making additional transfers to individuals. Thus, the overall impact of federal spending on the allocation of resources between private and public use will depend not only on how much federal spending is in the form of purchases of goods and services, but also on how much of grants-in-aid to state and local governments are used for state and local purchases. Likewise, the total redistributional effect of federal spending must encompass that portion of state and local government transfers financed by the federal government as well as the transfers made by the federal government itself.

The functional breakdown of federal expenditures discloses some interesting facts. Defense spending is no longer the largest item in the budget. It now occupies second place, trailing behind outlays on income security. Income security payments—old age, survivors, and disability benefit payments, unemployment compensation, public assistance, and other income supplements—account for about 36 percent of the total. Defense is next with about 26 percent of the total. If net interest payments of $23.5 billion are added to national defense and income security payments, these items alone account for 69 percent of total spending—some $246 billion in 1975. All the other programs of the federal government—foreign affairs, space and energy research, health, postal services, agriculture, natural resources, transportation, veterans' benefits, education, revenue sharing, general government, and so on—make up only 31 percent of total spending.

How can one decide what the federal government *should* do in each of these areas? And how is one to judge the government's actual performance?

Federal versus State and Local Responsibility

First, what types of programs come under the responsibility of the federal government rather than the authority of the states and their subdivisions must be considered. The legal division of responsibility among the various levels of government is found in the Constitution and in court interpretations of the Constitution. The Constitution divides the powers of government: those of the national government are specified in Article I, Section 8, while those of the states and their subdivisions are residual. The Tenth Amendment reserves to the states all powers not granted to the national government or prohibited to the states. The federal government, through Congress, was given the power to levy and collect taxes, duties, imposts, and excises, to pay the debts and provide for the common defense and general welfare of the United States, a provision which was intended to restrict the scope of federal activity.[1] There is no specific mention of spending for highways, public health, education, or public welfare, here or anywhere else in the Constitution; and since the Tenth Amendment does not deny these powers to the states, they are presumed to be residual powers of the states.

Until the 1930s the courts were reluctant to allow the national government to assume powers beyond those necessary to provide for national defense and to regulate interstate trade and commerce, and the Congress was generally reluctant to seek new responsibilities. As

1. See James A. Maxwell and J. Richard Aronson, *Financing State and Local Governments* (3d ed., Brookings Institution, 1977), chap. 1, esp. p. 12.

Table 8-1. Federal Expenditures, by Object, Function, and Type, 1975

Amounts in billions of dollars

Object and function	Purchases of goods and services	Transfer payments and net interest paid	Grants-in-aid to state and local governments	Subsidies less current surplus of government enterprises	Total	Percentage of total
Public goods						
National defense	84.3	6.7	0.4	−0.1	91.2	25.5
Space research and technology	3.7	...	0.1	...	3.8	1.1
General government, except net interest paid	6.4	7.7	0.4	−0.2	14.4	4.0
International affairs and finance	1.3	3.1	...	*	4.4	1.2
Subtotal	95.7	17.5	0.9	−0.3	113.7	31.8
Semipublic goods						
Health and hospitals	3.6	1.5	2.6	...	7.6	2.1
Education	1.3	1.7	7.0	...	10.1	2.8
Transportation	3.2	3.4	5.9	1.0	13.5	3.8
Regulation of commerce and finance[a]	1.4	*	*	*	1.5	0.4
Postal services	0.7	...	...	3.2	3.9	1.1
Civilian safety	0.2	*	0.6	...	0.8	0.2
Natural resources	5.1	*	0.6	−0.6	5.1	1.4

Nuclear energy research and development	1.6	...	0.2	*	1.9	0.5
Utilities and sanitation	*	...	3.4	0.2	3.6	1.0
Subtotal	17.3	6.7	20.4	3.7	48.1	13.4
Income redistribution						
Public assistance and relief	*	4.5	15.3	*	19.8	5.5
Old age, survivors, and disability benefits	0.9	65.9	0.2	...	67.0	18.7
Other social security and special welfare services	2.0	22.6	2.2	*	26.7	7.5
Labor	1.0	0.1	5.7	...	6.8	1.9
Veterans' benefits and services	4.3	14.3	0.1	*	18.6	5.2
Agriculture and agricultural resources	2.0	*	0.6	1.0	3.6	1.0
Unemployment benefits	*	17.3	...	...	17.3	4.8
Housing and community development	1.3	0.1	3.0	2.1	6.5	1.8
Subtotal	11.4	124.7	27.0	3.1	166.3	46.5
Net interest paid	...	23.5	...	...	23.5	6.6
General revenue sharing	...	...	6.1	...	6.1	1.7
Total expenditures[b]	124.4	172.4	54.4	6.5	357.8	100.0

Sources: U.S. Department of Commerce, *Survey of Current Business*, vol. 56 (July 1976), p. 41. Figures are rounded.

* 0.05 or less.

a. Includes function entitled "other commerce and transportation."

b. Includes employee compensation on a disbursement basis. The figures by type of function include employee compensation on an accrual basis.

a result, in 1927 the federal government accounted for less than one-fifth of total government expenditures for civilian purposes—some 17 percent.[2]

However, during the 1930s, with the problems and pressures of the greatest economic depression in U.S. history, there developed a shift in social philosophy and judicial thinking. The judicial interpretation of the Constitution that emerged in the 1930s "accepted a reading of the general welfare clause that places no discernible judicial limits on the amounts or purposes of Federal spending."[3] By 1938 the federal share of civilian expenditures had risen to more than 40 percent, and has remained above 35 percent since that time.[4] In short, the powers of the national government to tax and spend have come to be interpreted very broadly indeed and now cover many areas of spending formerly reserved exclusively to the states and their subdivisions, among them public welfare, work relief, and public health. There are generally no precise legal boundaries to the areas of responsibility of the various levels of government.[5]

The division of responsibility for spending and taxation among levels of government is now a question mainly for legislative and executive judgment. Such judgment generally employs at least two criteria. One of these is efficiency. Congress and the President nearly always consider whether a particular program can be carried out most efficiently at the federal level or at some other level. Some activities, such as sewage treatment and garbage disposal, can clearly be performed most efficiently at the local (sometimes the county) level. Others, such as policing of highway traffic, can be most efficiently performed by state governments. Still others, like national defense and postal service, can be carried out most efficiently by the federal government. Aside from these areas, about which there is little dispute, there is a host of activities, including education, medical care for the aged, public health, and welfare payments, about which there can be differences of opinion on the level of government that can most efficiently provide the service.

2. Ibid., p. 16.
3. U.S. Commission on Intergovernmental Relations, *A Report to the President* (The Commission, 1955), p. 29, quoted in ibid., p. 19.
4. Maxwell and Aronson, *Financing State and Local Governments*, p. 16 (figure 1-1, lower panel).
5. There are exceptions to this statement. For example, the provision of police protection is a responsibility still reserved to the states.

Another criterion is political ideology. Many fear expansion of federal activity, for example, because they believe individual freedom, liberty, and political participation are best preserved by keeping government activities at the lowest level of government. In this view, keeping most government activities at the local level provides for closer contact among the persons receiving the services, those paying the taxes, and the officials who make policy and administer the programs. Transfer of these activities, or portions of them, to higher government levels may mean that decisions are no longer made by officials familiar with the circumstances, needs, and desires of those affected.

These two criteria—efficiency and decentralization of decisions—often conflict. A particular program might be most efficiently administered at the federal level, but it might also create, in the minds of many, an undesirable concentration of power at that level. In such cases, the public must choose its preferred alternative through its elected representatives.

The question, what level of government should carry out a particular program, should be distinguished from the question, what level of government should raise revenue. Society may decide, for example, that education is best carried out at the state and local levels but that it should be financed with federal funds. In the past three decades, many state and local programs have been partially or wholly federally financed through the grant-in-aid mechanism. These programs may be strictly regulated and controlled by the federal government through a set of standards and requirements imposed on the states and localities receiving the funds; or, on the other hand, the amount of federal control may be minimal.

The fact that the federal tax system is quite efficient in raising revenues led to a number of proposals during the 1960s to make block grants-in-aid to states, to refund a portion of federal revenues raised in each state to the state and its subdivisions, or to share federal tax revenues on some formula basis with state and local governments.[6] The federal revenue sharing program, which was enacted in

6. For discussions on revenue sharing, see Joseph A. Pechman, "Financing State and Local Government," in American Bankers Association, *Proceedings of a Symposium on Federal Taxation* (ABA, 1965) (Brookings Reprint 103); Walter W. Heller, *New Dimensions of Political Economy* (Norton, 1967), chap. 3; and Walter W. Heller and Joseph A. Pechman, "Questions and Answers on Revenue Sharing," in *Revenue Sharing and Its Alternatives: What Future for Fiscal Federalism?* Hearings before the Subcommittee on Fiscal Policy of the Joint Economic Committee, 90:1

1972, reflects both the superior ability of the federal government to raise revenue and the need to decentralize the decisionmaking processes of the federal government.

The State and Local Fiscal Assistance Act of 1972 appropriated $30 billion in federal funds to 39,000 state and local governments during the five-year period 1972–76. Revenue sharing funds were made available to these states and localities with minimal federal restrictions and controls, thus allowing regional and local decisionmakers to apply the funds to their own needs. The success of the revenue sharing experience in decentralizing the decisionmaking process on the one hand, and in supplementing the revenue needs of states and localities on the other, was a major force in the call for its renewal. The revenue sharing act was extended in 1976 through September 30, 1980, with increases in outlays to a rate of $6.85 billion a year.

Economists have not thoroughly investigated the criteria for determining the proper governmental level for financing programs. One important consideration, however, would seem to be the extent to which the benefits from state and local programs are national as well as local in nature; that is, the extent to which benefits "spill over" and benefit the nation as a whole as well as the states and localities. Beyond this, about all that can be said is that the two criteria mentioned above for determining the proper level of government to be involved in providing particular programs also apply in some degree to questions on the source of financing. Whether programs are financed by the federal government or by state and local governments will have considerable bearing on the degree of decentralization of governmental activities. The source of revenue may also affect the efficiency with which programs are carried out.

For the purposes of the remainder of this chapter, however, it will be assumed that the crucial issue of the division of responsibility between the federal government and the states for programs and financing is resolved. That is, suppose the federal government has certain clearly defined areas of responsibility. How big should the federal budget be? How much should the federal government spend on national defense? On education? On old-age assistance?

(GPO, 1967), pp. 111–17 (Brookings Reprint 135); for a more recent discussion of revenue sharing, see Richard P. Nathan, Allen D. Manvel, and Susannah E. Calkins, *Monitoring Revenue Sharing* (Brookings Institution, 1975).

Spending on Public Goods

Consider the federal spending programs for public goods in table 8-1—national defense, space research and technology, general government (except net interest), and international affairs. This group of federal expenditures amounted to $113.7 billion in 1975. Of this total, $95.7 billion was for purchases of goods and services, and $17.5 billion was for transfer payments, mainly retirement allowances. Grants-in-aid and subsidies were negligible.

As table 8-1 shows, this group accounted for 32 percent of total federal expenditures in 1975. The goods and services included in this group are clearly of the kinds that, if they were not provided by government, would not be provided at all.

The basic characteristic of public goods is that they are available to society as a whole and are independent of each individual's tax contributions. The best example of a public good is national defense. Every citizen of the United States benefits to some degree from the security provided by the armed forces, regardless of what share of the cost he or she may bear. Another characteristic of public goods and services is that, unlike private goods, their use by any one individual or group does not reduce the amount available for any other individual or group. Since their benefits accrue to society as a whole, a market price for units of the public good or service cannot possibly be established. What price should the government charge the individual for the provision of nuclear submarines and army divisions? Society collectively pays for public goods, usually through general taxation.

In the attempt to determine the level of federal spending on public goods, the following questions are usually raised. First, how much of society's resources should be devoted to the production of public goods for which the federal government is responsible? Second, how much should be spent on defense as compared with, say, international affairs and the space program—that is, how should the public goods' budget be allocated among the various goods and services? Finally, given a specific budget for the provision of a certain public good (for example, the defense budget), how should the total amount be allocated among alternative means of accomplishing the goal of national security?

The first of these questions is the most difficult to answer. Societies face scarcity, the scarcity of resources as compared with wants. Thus, members of society have to assess the relative benefits of alternative uses of resources. For example, if they decide to devote a portion of their resources to space exploration so that a space shuttle between earth and other planets becomes possible, they must give up the use of that portion for other purposes; they must be satisfied with fewer television sets, cars, boats, and the like. Since the provision of public goods requires that resources be diverted from private to public use, some criterion is needed for deciding on the proper level of spending on public goods. If some basis could be found for evaluating the benefits and costs to society of public, as well as private, goods, a comparison of these benefits and costs might provide such a criterion. Theoretically, benefit-cost comparisons could be used to determine the optimal level of spending on public goods.

Unfortunately, the task of estimating society's benefits and costs from each unit of federal expenditure on public goods is difficult.[7] As an example, consider defense expenditures again. How can the additional benefits to society from additional units of defense, such as one more nuclear submarine, be estimated? The cost to society of providing an additional nuclear submarine is that quantity of private goods and services (refrigerators, television sets, and so on) that must be given up in order to provide the resources for the submarine. As important as certain private goods may be, there is no way to tell whether society's benefits from an additional nuclear submarine exceed or fall short of society's costs (the benefits forgone) in giving up these private goods.

Furthermore, how can one compare society's benefits from expenditures on submarines to expenditures on food or entertainment when benefits from submarines extend for several years in the future. When future as well as current benefits are involved, some form of discounting of future benefits to the present has to take place before any comparison can be made. That is, society must ascertain the present value (as of the time of the expenditure) of the future worth of each public activity. Here again, unfortunately, difficulties arise: what is the appropriate discount rate for public projects?[8] The prevailing wisdom

7. A review of cost-benefit analysis, its applicability and shortcomings, is given in Peter O. Steiner, "Public Expenditure Budgeting," in Alan S. Blinder and others, *The Economics of Public Finance* (Brookings Institution, 1974), pp. 313–31.

8. For a detailed discussion on the discount rate for public projects, see A. R. Prest and R. Turvey, "Cost-Benefit Analysis: A Survey," in *Surveys of Economic Theory,* vol. 3 (St. Martin's Press, 1967), pp. 155–207.

on this point is that the discount rate should reflect the rate of return that can be earned on those resources had they been left in private use; this is called the "opportunity cost" of resources. Second, it should reflect the willingness of society to forgo the use of resources for current consumption in exchange for future benefits (or consumption); this is called the "rate of time preference."

Economists have estimated that in the late 1960s the social discount rate ranged between 8 and 13 percent in real terms.[9] In most cost-benefit analyses carried out by the government, however, a rate of 3 to 5 percent was used. If the higher estimates are more realistic, some public projects that are not worth their cost are now being undertaken and undue favoritism is shown toward long-lived projects.

The second question—how much should be spent on alternative public goods—entails a comparison of the benefits and costs of one public good with those of another. Given the overall level of federal spending on public goods, the essential comparison here is between the benefits derived from the last dollar spent on one public good and the last dollar spent on another. This involves a basic economic criterion, that expenditures on a good or service should be continued only to the point where the benefit derived from the last dollar spent is equalized with the benefit of the last dollar spent on other goods or services. As far as spending on public goods is concerned, when the benefits from the last dollar spent on one public good (for example, defense) fall short of those derived from another public good (for example, international affairs), funds should be reallocated to the latter good to achieve a higher total gain for society.

A simple example may help to illustrate this point. Suppose that society has already decided to spend $50 billion on public goods at the federal level, and that the only public goods to be provided are defense and international affairs. How much should be spent on defense and how much on international affairs? Clearly, the first thing to be identified is the goal to be achieved in each case. Once such goals are identified and their worth calculated, fewer dollars should be devoted to defense, for example, if the benefits derived from some defense activities are less than the benefits derived from an equivalent amount of dollars spent on international affairs. The total budget should be

9. For a discussion of the various methods used by economists in estimating the 8–13 percent range of the social rate of discount, see J. A. Seagraves, "More on the Social Rate of Discount," *Quarterly Journal of Economics*, vol. 84 (August 1970), pp. 430–50.

allocated between defense and international affairs in such a way that the benefit to society from the last dollar spent on both activities is equalized.

But it is really not feasible to apply such a criterion. In the area of public goods, economic criteria offer little guidance in determining the total level of federal spending and in choosing between alternative uses because the benefit side of cost-benefit analysis collapses. As Richard A. Musgrave put it: "Cost-benefit analysis provides no substitute for the basic problem of evaluation in the case of final social goods. All it can do is to expedite efficient decision-making after the basic problem of evaluation is solved."[10]

The final question—how should expenditures be allocated among alternative means of achieving a given goal—is less difficult to answer. In fact, this is the area where systems analysis, in particular cost-effectiveness analysis, has been successfully applied. Systems analysis is concerned with the discovery and specification of objectives and the evaluation of alternative means of reaching these objectives. It was first introduced into the federal government in 1961 in the decisionmaking process in the Department of Defense. During the mid-1960s, it was embodied in the program planning system and applied to all other federal programs. Since the demise of the program planning system during the Nixon administration, this method of analysis has been sharply curtailed.

Cost-effectiveness is a method for evaluating the various means available to achieve the most for a given cost or a given objective for the least cost. The application and usefulness of cost-effectiveness analysis can be illustrated by some examples in the area of defense.[11]

Suppose that the decisionmaker is concerned with the allocation of the portion of the national defense budget earmarked for improving offensive forces, fixed at $A billion. He can use this amount for either the procurement of additional Minuteman missiles or additional Polaris submarines, and his objective will be to maximize the total offensive capability of the given budget. For each alternative force, a quantitative estimate of costs and expected military benefits (effectiveness) must thus be made. Suppose that the effectiveness of

10. "Cost-Benefit Analysis and the Theory of Public Finance," *Journal of Economic Literature,* vol. 7 (September 1969), p. 800.
11. For a discussion of the use of cost-effectiveness in the area of defense, see Charles J. Hitch, *Decision-Making for Defense* (University of California Press, 1965), pp. 43–58.

each force can be measured by a single number—for example, the expected number of enemy troops that can be killed or targets destroyed. Then if all the $A billion is spent on Minuteman squadrons, X number of enemy or targets will be the offensive capability, while, if the $A billion is spent on Polaris submarines, Y number of enemy or targets will be the capability. A clear-cut choice can thus be made in favor of the Minuteman if X is greater than Y because that choice will maximize the effectiveness of the given defense budget.

This example illustrates one aspect of cost-effectiveness, the goal of obtaining the most output from a given budget. Consider another defense example, which illustrates how a given objective may be achieved with the least cost.[12] Suppose a defense objective is to be able to destroy 97 out of 100 enemy targets, using missiles each of which has a 50 percent chance of destroying a single target. That is, if 100 missiles are fired, 50 targets will be destroyed; if a second 100 are fired, 25 of the 50 targets left will be destroyed, or a total of 75. Firing 300 will destroy about 87 targets, 400 will destroy 94 targets, and 500 will destroy 97 targets. In this case, a 97 percent goal can be achieved at a minimum cost of 500 missiles, fired at the same time.

An important aspect of cost-effectiveness analysis is that, although it makes the policymaker's choices explicit, it does not itself make the correct choice obvious. In the previous example, the first 100 missiles accomplish 50 kills, while the last 100 missiles increase the destruction capability by only 3 kills (from 94 kills to 97 kills). Does such a small increase in destructive capability justify the cost of the last 100 missiles? The decisionmaker in the Department of Defense must then decide whether the additional output (3 kills) is worth the additional cost of the last 100 missiles. By bringing such information to his attention, cost-effectiveness analysis can contribute a great deal to shaping the decisionmaker's judgment. In short, while not making the decision, this method sorts out the factors that need to be taken into account when a decision is made.

Spending on Semipublic Goods

Consider the federal expenditures grouped together in the second section of table 8-1. This $48 billion represents expenditures on what may be called semipublic goods. This type of spending is relatively

12. Ibid., pp. 50–51.

small at the federal level (accounting for less than 15 percent of federal expenditures in 1975), but it is a very large part of state and local government expenditures. Semipublic goods are goods and services that benefit specific individual users but also benefit society as a whole. Take, for example, the case of education. Education expenditures yield a direct benefit to the user in the form of a higher expected life income and an indirect benefit to society as a whole in the form of a better environment for innovations, better qualified voters, better health, a reduction in the crime rate, and so on. The private benefits of a semipublic good can be supplied by private producers in a free market economy, as in the case of private schools and colleges, but since education provides extra benefits to society, the government may be called upon to supplement the amount of education supplied by the private market.

Education as a semipublic good is provided mostly by state and local governments, in the form of public schools, colleges, and universities. The federal government, however, contributes to state and local government spending on education through its grants-in-aid. As table 8-1 shows, 70 percent of federal spending on education is in this form. In addition, the federal government provides aid to education for areas affected by federal installations, loans and grants to college students, and other services.

To determine how much the government should spend on semipublic goods, the benefits accruing to the individual and to the nation must be identified and compared with their costs.[13] Although the private element of benefits lends itself to cost-benefit analysis, benefit calculation is not feasible for the public element. Furthermore, lack of reliable statistical data on private benefits and the difficulty of quantifying the social elements of costs have prevented (at least for the present) the use of cost-benefit analysis in determining the total

13. Cost-benefit analysis originated as an administrative device adapted to a strictly limited type of federal activity, the improvement of navigation. A river and harbor act in 1902 required a board of engineers to study the desirability of Army Corps of Engineers river and harbor projects in terms of the benefits to commerce and the cost. The Flood Control Act of 1936 is another example of the application of cost-benefit analysis to government projects. For early application of the concept, see R. J. Hammond, *Benefit-Cost Analysis and Water-Pollution Control* (Stanford University, Food Research Institute, 1960), and Robert Dorfman, ed., *Measuring Benefits of Government Investments* (Brookings Institution, 1965). For an evaluation of its application and use by federal agencies, see Alice M. Rivlin, *Systematic Thinking for Social Action* (Brookings Institution, 1971).

budget for semipublic goods. As it now stands, the level of spending is determined through the political process.

However, cost-benefit analysis, even when based on arbitrary calculation of benefits and costs, is sometimes helpful in evaluating the merits of existing federal programs as well as in evaluating proposals for new programs involving semipublic goods. The first step in cost-benefit calculation is to resolve the following basic issues: which costs and which benefits should be included; how are they to be valued; at what interest rate are they to be discounted? Once these issues are resolved the calculation is straightforward, as illustrated in the following example.

Suppose that the program to be evaluated is designed to reduce the number of high school dropouts.[14] The goal, then, is to determine whether, on the basis of the expected benefits and costs, the program is worthwhile. The starting point in the calculation is a projection of the output—in this case, the number of dropouts prevented either in each year of the program or in some typical year of its operation. Next, the return (benefits) from dropout prevention must be estimated. Since dropout prevention, a semipublic good, yields benefits directly to the individual as well as to society as a whole, two types of benefits have to be estimated. The individual benefit can be estimated by computing the present value of additional lifetime income that the student may expect. The benefit to society is more difficult to estimate since a dollar figure (with due allowance for discounting) must be assigned to the effect of dropout prevention on such factors as crime and delinquency, the unemployment rate, transfer payments (such as unemployment compensation), and tax revenues. Thus, for this program, only an approximate measure of society's benefits can be estimated.

After a dollar figure has been computed for the total benefit, a similar procedure must be followed to estimate the full cost of the program—that is, the actual resources that will be needed to finance it. The rest is simple; the benefits are the numerator, the costs are the denominator, and the result is the benefit-cost ratio. If this ratio is greater than one—that is, if benefits exceed costs—the program is worthwhile; otherwise it should not be undertaken. The higher the

14. For a cost-benefit analysis of a specific program designed to reduce high school dropouts, see Burton A. Weisbrod, "Preventing High School Dropouts," in Dorfman, ed., *Measuring Benefits of Government Investments,* pp. 117–49.

ratio, the greater the payoff. Alternative programs can be ranked according to their benefit-cost ratios to facilitate the decisionmaker's choice among them. Clearly, a program with a ratio of 9:1 is to be preferred to a program with a ratio of 4:1.

The danger of accepting without reservations the dollar magnitudes produced by cost-benefit analyses cannot be overstressed. Serious difficulties are present in quantifying benefits as well as costs and in choosing the appropriate discount rate for alternative programs.[15]

Spending to Affect Income Distribution

In addition to government programs for the purposes noted so far, federal government spending and taxation also arise out of efforts to promote equity in the distribution of income among persons and regions. The federal expenditures in the third section of table 8-1 were designed primarily for this purpose. As can be seen from the table, this type of spending bulks very large in the federal budget; it represented 46 percent of total expenditures in 1975. In that year, of the $166 billion of federal spending on the items in this group, $125 billion was in the form of transfer payments; $27 billion was for grants-in-aid to state and local governments (for public assistance, relief, and welfare), $3 billion was for subsidies (less the current surplus of government enterprises), and $11 billion represented purchases of goods and services.

In our society, the government's budget affects the distribution of income in two ways. First, when government taxes and spends, it usually alters the distribution of income to some extent, whether or not such an objective was intended. When, for example, a contract is awarded to a business firm to build submarines, the government's primary objective is a stronger defense posture. Nevertheless, this expenditure, and the way in which it is financed, probably will have some effect on the distribution of income. The business firm to which the contract is awarded, and also its suppliers of materials and labor, will benefit directly in terms of work opportunities, income, and profits.

The second way in which government spending and taxation affect the distribution of income is through programs specifically designed

15. See the various papers in Samuel B. Chase, Jr., ed., *Problems in Public Expenditure Analysis* (Brookings Institution, 1968).

for that purpose, such as federal spending on public housing, medical services, social security and veterans' benefits, and public assistance and relief, which are undertaken especially for the benefit of certain individuals or groups, mostly the poor, the aged, or those in distressed circumstances for economic or other reasons. Although the benefit derived from this type of spending may accrue to all individuals in the society, particular groups of individuals benefit more than others.

In this area as well as in the areas of public and semipublic goods, cost-effectiveness analysis may be performed to evaluate the relative merits of alternative programs designed to accomplish the same goals. For example, cost-effectiveness may be used to determine whether, in the alleviation of poverty, a negative income tax is superior to a jobs program of the same magnitude.[16]

Taxation may also be used specifically to redistribute income. The government may design a tax structure (a combination of income, gift, death, and other taxes) to achieve this objective. Alternatively, the government may interfere directly (not through spending or taxation) in the determination of income in the private market by imposing minimum wages or subsidizing the prices of certain services or products.

It would be inaccurate to say that the executive branch or the majority of Congress has carefully formulated any overall view of how income should be distributed. Decisions on specific proposals in the areas listed above, however, all involve implicit judgments on a desirable distribution of income. Unanimity of opinion about what is "fair" or "equitable" may be impossible to attain, since fairness does not necessarily mean the same thing for everyone in our society, for every society, or for the same society at every moment in time. Nevertheless, some guidelines are probably supported by a majority, and fairly widespread agreement is often reached on specific programs.

Given a goal of a particular pattern of income distribution, the federal government will set transfers and taxes to achieve that goal. That is, the initial allocation of wealth and income generated by private markets and the effects on distribution of federal spending

16. For an explanation of the negative income tax idea, see Joseph A. Pechman, *Federal Tax Policy* (3d ed., Brookings Institution, 1977), pp. 77–83; Christopher Green, *Negative Taxes and the Poverty Problem* (Brookings Institution, 1967); and Joseph A. Pechman and P. Michael Timpane, eds., *Work Incentives and Income Guarantees: The New Jersey Negative Income Tax Experiment* (Brookings Institution, 1975).

and taxing for other purposes (such as the production of public goods) are the background to determining the amount of government transfers and taxes required to achieve the desired distribution pattern. The specific amount will depend on what the desired distribution is and how different it is from the existing distribution.

Other Federal Spending

The last two items in table 8-1 consist of net interest paid and general revenue sharing. In 1975, interest paid on its debt to the public by the federal government accounted for 7 percent of federal expenditures. Since the debt was incurred mostly as the result of past wars and recessions, it has something of the character of a defense expenditure or of an expenditure that represents in part the cost to the government of stabilizing the economy. In the use of society's resources, it is similar to transfer payments but without an explicit distributional consideration. General revenue sharing accounted for a little less than 2 percent of total federal expenditures in 1975. Since it represents a form of unconditional grant to state and local governments, it could have distributional as well as resource allocative impact, depending on the way the governmental units choose to spend these funds.

The Role of the Individual in Determining the Level of Federal Spending

So far the criteria by which federal spending should be determined have been discussed. But what about actual spending? And to what extent does the decisionmaking process of the federal government reflect the choice and preferences of its citizens?

As seen in chapter 3, the actual level of federal spending is determined through the budget-making process of both the executive branch and the Congress. In the earlier phases of the budget process, most federal agencies attempt to use some form of systems analysis in the planning and preparation stages of their program. The final outcome—the total budget dollar—as well as its allocation among the various functions is, however, determined by the political process. The individual citizen's role in this process is very limited. Individuals do not directly participate in the budget-making process; they do not vote on expenditures or tax legislation (although some individuals express their views on budget matters during congressional hearings) but can only influence the decisionmaking process and the final outcome through their elected representatives.

How successful is this method of representation in reflecting society's preferences? There are essentially two views concerning the nature and means for articulating the public interest.[17] In one view, the political process functions as a marketlike mechanism in representing the views of the members of society. In this case direct voting by individuals on budget matters would signal to policymakers citizens' wishes, just as the market mechanism functions in the private economy. The government, in this view, is a decisionmaker only to the extent that it reacts to and carries out the proposals given in those signals it receives.

The second view holds that while individual preferences clearly exist, they are so ambiguous or conflicting that the political process is required to forge a public interest. Accordingly, the government is the decisionmaker, with the role of individuals limited to constraining the decisionmakers.

Clearly, whether one adheres to the first or the second of these views, public policy decisions cannot be made in a vacuum. The life of any government is only as long as its constituents are willing to endure; governments and elected representatives cannot remain in office if the wishes and preferences of those they represent are entirely disregarded. In the United States today, there is a strong collective preference for certain public functions and dislike for others. Agreement on government spending may not be unanimous, but presumably the outcome of the budget process—even though it does not allow for individual direct participation—captures the collective view and thus represents the preferences of the majority.

Some Common Fallacies in Judging Federal Spending

Several arguments have been made against or in support of federal expenditures and taxation. One frequently heard argument against government spending is that by its very nature government is less efficient than the private sector in providing goods and services. Pri-

17. For a detailed discussion on these views, see Steiner, "Public Expenditure Budgeting," pp. 269–82.

vate firms, it is claimed, are relatively free of the bureaucratic red tape and political maneuvering that make for inefficiency. And since private production is carried on at closer to the minimum feasible cost than public production, the production of goods and services should generally be left in private hands.

Whether government production of goods and services is in fact inefficient might well be debated. Efficiency aside, however, there are two weaknesses in this argument. One is that it confuses production with spending. Over half of federal spending on goods and services is for goods produced by private firms; most of the rest consists of payment for services of government employees. In other words, for the most part, government is not in competition with private industry. The second weakness in this argument is that there is no use in showing that private producers are more efficient than the government if private producers are unable or unwilling to provide the goods and services in question. This is the case with defense, space exploration, international affairs, and so on. In short, government spending on public goods is spending that cannot or will not be duplicated by the private sector. To eliminate defense spending because it is wastefully administered and to let people buy more cars instead resembles, as one observer put it, the action taken by a "man in Atlanta who wanted to go to New Orleans but decided to take the train to New York because it was faster."[18] This is not to say that we should be tolerant of waste in the administration of government programs. The lack of a profit incentive can make inefficiency a serious problem. But if these programs are meeting public wants, as expressed through the political process, a demonstration of waste in the programs is an argument for eliminating waste, not for eliminating the programs.

Another argument against government spending states that the taxes required to pay for government expenditures distort the choices of consumers and producers by causing the market prices of goods, as well as of the factors of production, to diverge from what they would have been in the absence of these taxes. This divergence, it is said, involves a dead-weight loss of efficiency in the production of private goods. The answer to this argument would again be that, though waste engendered by a bad tax system is real and significant, it does not constitute an argument against federal spending. For if such expenditures were eliminated, the market economy would not

18. Francis M. Bator, *The Question of Government Spending: Public Needs and Private Wants* (Harper, 1960), p. 103.

itself provide the public goods or transfer payments. Taxes ought to be considered in estimating the benefits and costs of government programs, but the existence of costs of tax collection, of tax distortion, or of any other burden of the tax structure means not that the program is not worthwhile but that the tax structure should be changed.

There are also some fallacies in the arguments commonly used to support more government spending. Quite often, for example, government expenditures are compared with GNP, and it is implied that in some sense a rise in government spending is justified by a rise in GNP or that government spending should rise in step with GNP. While such a comparison may provide a measure of the relative importance of government in the economy, it is no criterion for judging the desirable level of government expenditures. This level should be gauged as far as possible on the basis of costs and benefits to society from the use of resources in the private sector as against their use in the public sector. Thus, the relation of government spending to GNP does not by itself provide a useful criterion for evaluating the level of federal expenditures.

It is also misleading to judge federal expenditures solely with reference to fiscal policy. When there is unemployment, there may be strong pressure for increased spending, since the opportunity cost of increased government expenditures is very low. But, even though resources are unemployed, federal expenditures must still be judged on grounds of efficiency. There is usually no justification for make-work spending just to reduce unemployment. Tax cuts should be considered as an alternative to increased federal spending.

These examples of rules of thumb and the faulty reasoning behind each could be extended almost indefinitely. Statements such as "when defense spending goes up, nondefense spending should go down by an equal amount," or "government spending is generally wasteful," reflect a misunderstanding of the function of government spending and taxation, a misunderstanding that, it is to be hoped, has been corrected at least to some extent by this chapter.

Summary

Federal expenditures arise from the public's desire for public and semipublic goods—those that are not provided at all, or are provided inadequately, by the private market—and from efforts to achieve equity in the distribution of income. There are no precise economic rules or guidelines for judging the proper amount of expenditure for each of these purposes. For some federal programs, however—particularly in the area of semipublic goods such as health, education, and natural resource development—an estimate of costs and benefits of projects can be helpful in determining the proper amount of expenditure. For other programs—particularly in the area of public goods such as defense, international affairs, and redistribution of income—cost-benefit analysis cannot readily be applied. In the latter cases, federal expenditure policy turns largely on the citizenry's preferences for federal or for state and local responsibility, for public or for private goods, and the desired degree of redistribution of income. After programs have been chosen through the political process, however, and the total level of spending decided upon, cost-benefit and cost-effectiveness analysis can often guide the policymaker in choosing among alternative programs, and in evaluating the relative merits of new as well as existing programs.

APPENDIX A

Statistical Tables

Table A-1. Summary of Federal Budget Operations, Fiscal Years 1967–76
Billions of dollars

	Total budget			Means of financing			Outstanding debt[a]	
Fiscal year	Net receipts	Net expenditures	Surplus or deficit (−)	Borrowing from the public	Reduction in cash and monetary assets	Total financing	Gross	Held by the public
1967	149.6	158.3	−8.7	2.8	5.9	8.7	341.3	267.5
1968	153.7	178.8	−25.2	23.1	2.1	25.2	369.8	290.6
1969	187.8	184.5	3.2	−11.1	14.4	−3.2	367.1	279.5
1970	193.7	196.6	−2.8	5.4	−2.6	2.8	382.6	284.9
1971	188.4	211.4	−23.0	19.4	3.6	23.0	409.5	304.3
1972	208.6	231.9	−23.2	19.4	3.8	23.2	437.3	323.8
1973	232.2	246.5	−14.3	19.3	−5.0	14.3	468.4	343.0
1974	264.9	268.4	−3.5	3.0	0.5	3.5	486.2	346.1
1975	281.0	324.6	−43.6	50.9	−7.2	43.6	544.1	396.9
1976	300.0	365.6	−65.6	82.8	−17.2	65.6	631.3	479.7

Sources: *Treasury Bulletin*, January 1977 and June 1976. Figures are rounded.
a. End of fiscal year. Since July 31, 1974, public debt outstanding has been adjusted to exclude the notes of the International Monetary Fund to conform with the presentation in the budget documents.

Table A-2. Budget Receipts by Source, Fiscal Years 1967-76

Millions of dollars

Source	1967	1968	1969	1970	1971	1972	1973	1974	1975	1976
Individual income taxes	61,526	68,726	87,249	90,412	86,230	94,737	103,246	118,952	122,386	131,603
Corporation income taxes	33,971	28,665	36,678	32,829	26,785	32,166	36,153	38,620	40,621	41,409
Employment taxes	27,823	29,224	34,236	39,133	41,699	46,120	54,876	65,892	75,204	79,909
Unemployment insurance	3,659	3,346	3,328	3,464	3,674	4,357	6,051	6,837	6,771	8,054
Premiums for other insurance and retirement	1,867	2,052	2,353	2,701	3,205	3,437	3,614	4,051	4,466	4,752
Excise taxes	13,719	14,079	15,222	15,705	16,614	15,477	16,260	16,844	16,551	16,963
Estate and gift taxes	2,978	3,051	3,491	3,644	3,735	5,436	4,917	5,035	4,611	5,216
Customs duties	1,901	2,038	2,319	2,430	2,591	3,287	3,188	3,334	3,676	4,074
Other	2,108	2,491	2,908	3,424	3,858	3,633	3,921	5,369	6,711	8,026
Total	149,552	153,671	187,784	193,743	188,392	208,649	232,225	264,932	280,997	300,005

Sources: *The Budget of the United States Government, Fiscal Year 1978*, and *Fiscal Year 1977*. Figures are rounded.

Table A-3. Budget Outlays by Function, Fiscal Years 1967–76

Millions of dollars

Function	1967	1968	1969	1970	1971	1972	1973	1974	1975	1976
National defense	69,101	79,409	80,207	79,284	76,807	77,356	75,072	78,569	86,585	89,996
International affairs	4,695	4,612	3,784	3,564	3,093	3,868	3,504	4,821	5,862	5,067
General science, space, and technology	6,231	5,522	5,016	4,508	4,180	4,174	4,030	3,977	3,989	4,370
Agriculture	2,982	4,541	5,779	5,164	4,288	5,279	4,855	2,230	1,660	2,502
Natural resources, environment, and energy	3,697	4,010	3,901	4,043	4,941	5,521	5,947	6,571	9,537	11,282
Commerce and transportation	9,205	10,637	7,065	9,090	10,396	10,601	9,930	13,096	16,010	17,248
Community and regional development	1,412	1,891	2,224	3,166	3,632	4,325	5,529	4,911	4,431	5,300
Health	6,759	9,708	11,758	13,051	14,716	17,471	18,832	22,074	27,647	33,448
Education, training, employment, and social services	6,023	7,004	6,871	7,888	9,045	11,694	11,874	11,598	15,248	18,167
Veterans' benefits and services	6,899	6,882	7,640	8,677	9,776	10,730	12,013	13,386	16,597	18,432
Interest	12,533	13,751	15,793	18,312	19,609	20,582	22,813	28,072	30,974	34,589
General government	1,569	1,684	1,649	1,940	2,159	2,466	2,682	3,327	3,089	2,927
Income security	30,821	33,680	37,281	43,066	55,423	63,911	72,958	84,431	108,605	127,406
Law enforcement and justice	610	650	761	952	1,299	1,650	2,131	2,462	2,942	3,320
Revenue sharing and general purpose fiscal assistance	288	311	365	451	488	531	7,222	6,746	7,005	7,119
Undistributed offsetting receipts	−4,573	−5,460	−5,545	−6,567	−8,427	−8,137	−12,318	−16,651	−14,075	−14,704
Total	158,254	178,833	184,548	196,588	211,425	232,021	247,074	269,620	326,105	366,466

Sources: Same as table A-2.

Table A-4. Budget Outlays for Defense and Nondefense Purposes, Fiscal Years 1955–76
Billions of dollars

Fiscal year	Total	National defense	Nondefense			
			Total	Payments to individuals	Net interest	All other
1955	68.5	39.9	28.6	13.0	4.8	10.8
1956	70.5	39.8	30.7	13.8	5.1	11.8
1957	76.7	42.3	34.5	15.6	5.4	13.5
1958	82.6	43.8	38.8	19.4	5.6	13.7
1959	92.1	45.9	46.2	21.2	5.8	19.2
1960	92.2	45.2	47.0	22.9	6.9	17.2
1961	97.8	46.6	51.2	25.9	6.7	18.6
1962	106.8	50.4	56.4	27.1	6.9	22.4
1963	111.3	51.5	59.8	28.7	7.7	23.4
1964	118.6	52.7	65.8	29.7	8.2	27.9
1965	118.4	48.6	69.8	30.4	8.6	30.8
1966	134.7	55.9	78.8	34.3	9.4	35.1
1967	158.3	69.1	89.2	40.1	10.3	38.8
1968	178.8	79.4	99.4	45.9	11.1	42.4
1969	184.5	80.2	104.3	52.8	12.7	38.9
1970	196.6	79.3	117.3	59.8	14.4	43.1
1971	211.4	76.8	134.6	74.5	14.8	45.2
1972	232.0	77.4	154.7	85.3	15.5	53.9
1973	247.1	75.1	172.0	95.9	17.4	58.7
1974	269.6	78.6	191.1	111.1	21.5	58.5
1975	326.1	86.6	239.5	142.6	23.3	73.6
1976	366.5	90.0	276.5	167.3	26.8	82.3

Source: *The Budget of the United States Government, Fiscal Year 1978.* Figures are rounded.

Table A-5. Percentage Distribution of Budget Outlays for Defense and Nondefense Purposes, Fiscal Years 1955–76

Fiscal year	Total	National defense	Nondefense			
			Total	Payments to individuals	Net interest	All other
1955	100.0	58.2	41.8	19.0	7.0	15.8
1956	100.0	56.5	43.5	19.6	7.2	16.7
1957	100.0	55.1	45.0	20.3	7.0	17.6
1958	100.0	53.0	47.0	23.5	6.8	16.6
1959	100.0	49.8	50.2	23.0	6.3	20.8
1960	100.0	49.0	51.0	24.8	7.5	18.7
1961	100.0	47.6	52.4	26.5	6.9	19.0
1962	100.0	47.2	52.8	25.4	6.5	21.0
1963	100.0	46.3	53.7	25.8	6.9	21.0
1964	100.0	44.4	55.5	25.0	6.9	23.5
1965	100.0	41.0	59.0	25.7	7.3	26.0
1966	100.0	41.5	58.5	25.5	7.0	26.1
1967	100.0	43.7	56.3	25.3	6.5	24.5
1968	100.0	44.4	55.6	25.7	6.2	23.7
1969	100.0	43.5	56.5	28.6	6.9	21.1
1970	100.0	40.3	59.7	30.4	7.3	21.9
1971	100.0	36.3	63.7	35.2	7.0	21.4
1972	100.0	33.4	66.7	36.8	6.7	23.2
1973	100.0	30.4	69.6	38.8	7.0	23.8
1974	100.0	29.2	70.9	41.2	8.0	21.7
1975	100.0	26.6	73.4	43.7	7.1	22.6
1976	100.0	24.6	75.4	45.6	7.3	22.5

Source: Table A-4. Figures are rounded.

Table A-6. Federal Receipts in the National Income Accounts, by Source, 1929–76

Millions of dollars

Year	Personal tax and nontax receipts				Corporate profits tax accruals	Indirect business tax and nontax accruals				Contributions for social insurance
	Total[a]	Income taxes	Estate and gift taxes	Non-taxes		Total[b]	Excise taxes	Customs duties	Non-taxes	
1929	1,263	1,179	60	24	1,224	1,193	562	575	56	124
1930	1,134	1,045	60	29	744	1,045	535	454	56	124
1931	607	532	55	20	423	894	489	356	49	123
1932	331	285	30	16	328	924	633	248	43	125
1933	474	355	68	16	462	1,619	1,220	283	36	115
1934	595	440	127	13	644	2,181	1,761	291	37	121
1935	827	568	245	14	820	2,181	1,694	353	39	136
1936	1,130	732	381	17	1,252	2,251	1,687	387	39	391
1937	1,723	1,305	397	21	1,337	2,406	1,771	454	42	1,573
1938	1,635	1,230	385	20	895	2,216	1,702	342	45	1,734
1939	1,235	854	366	15	1,285	2,322	1,818	327	44	1,879
1940	1,364	1,012	336	16	2,635	2,627	2,109	305	46	2,015
1941	2,016	1,599	396	21	7,333	3,567	2,814	416	55	2,504
1942	4,668	4,040	465	42	11,065	4,049	3,358	295	67	3,161
1943	16,517	15,906	455	79	13,616	4,944	4,055	396	112	4,181
1944	17,536	16,797	557	108	12,484	6,171	5,217	363	219	4,817
1945	19,379	18,526	654	118	10,234	7,128	6,175	384	216	5,754
1946	17,166	16,343	725	97	8,642	7,791	7,202	489	100	5,506
1947	19,643	18,784	819	40	10,664	7,791	7,246	418	127	5,122
1948	18,973	18,054	885	34	11,750	7,970	7,436	392	142	4,525
1949	16,137	15,362	740	35	9,598	8,020	7,505	365	150	4,951

1950	18,090	17,415	643	32	17,155	8,860	8,200	534	126	5,930
1951	26,131	25,354	731	46	21,676	9,352	8,625	575	152	7,118
1952	31,031	30,141	837	53	18,573	10,296	9,572	564	160	7,417
1953	32,247	31,273	910	64	19,458	10,895	10,152	570	173	7,412
1954	28,998	28,027	908	63	16,851	9,733	8,981	544	208	8,156
1955	31,437	30,419	968	50	21,073	10,674	9,792	657	225	9,375
1956	35,170	33,847	1,268	55	20,949	11,245	10,267	721	257	10,621
1957	37,411	35,936	1,430	45	20,404	11,793	10,754	768	271	12,298
1958	36,786	35,410	1,329	47	17,960	11,498	10,397	825	276	12,418
1959	39,914	38,466	1,404	44	22,484	12,508	11,185	1,049	274	14,920
1960	43,644	41,844	1,759	41	21,447	13,429	12,035	1,066	328	17,621
1961	44,704	42,709	1,950	45	21,491	13,602	12,169	1,030	403	18,261
1962	48,635	46,531	2,054	50	22,470	14,606	12,972	1,202	432	20,476
1963	51,483	49,185	2,241	57	24,578	15,258	13,509	1,227	522	23,096
1964	48,626	46,001	2,567	58	26,141	16,173	14,158	1,318	697	23,973
1965	53,947	51,080	2,815	52	28,899	16,479	13,870	1,613	996	25,012
1966	61,696	58,602	3,046	48	31,428	15,598	12,642	1,869	1,087	33,121
1967	67,475	64,351	3,065	59	30,026	16,265	13,328	1,909	1,028	36,730
1968	79,648	76,478	3,128	42	36,278	18,001	14,701	2,258	1,042	40,812
1969	94,821	91,197	3,563	61	36,212	18,985	15,539	2,370	1,076	46,966
1970	92,219	88,449	3,682	88	30,813	19,298	15,694	2,484	1,120	49,728
1971	89,883	85,230	4,588	65	33,510	20,351	15,988	3,112	1,251	54,904
1972	108,188	102,692	5,361	135	36,560	19,969	15,609	2,997	1,363	62,754
1973	114,640	109,420	5,092	128	42,992	21,215	16,652	3,271	1,292	79,439
1974	131,159	126,249	4,795	115	45,630	21,673	16,554	3,658	1,461	89,750
1975	125,740	120,725	4,894	121	42,570	23,943	16,405	5,844	1,694	94,257
1976c	145,300	139,800	5,400	100	55,600	23,500	17,100	4,700	1,700	105,800

Sources: U.S. Bureau of Economic Analysis, *The National Income and Product Accounts of the United States, 1929–74: Statistical Tables* (Government Printing Office, 1977), and *Survey of Current Business*.

a. Includes dividend tax, 1933–34, and automobile use tax, 1942–45, not shown separately.

b. Includes capital stock tax, 1933–45, not shown separately.

c. Preliminary.

Table A-7. Federal Expenditures in the National Income Accounts, by Type, 1939–76

Millions of dollars

| Year | Purchases of goods and services | | Transfer payments | | Grants-in-aid to state and local govern-ments | Net interest paid |
	National defense	Non-defense	To U.S. residents	To foreign companies and former U.S. residents		
1939	1,235	3,941	1,254	27	988	617
1940	2,197	3,880	1,438	32	857	707
1941	13,740	3,207	1,379	−14	807	751
1942	49,360	2,624	1,422	90	888	981
1943	79,741	1,608	1,241	−53	942	1,552
1944	87,432	1,958	1,842	−88	947	2,071
1945	73,502	1,123	4,315	352	870	2,924
1946	14,789	2,828	9,125	2,249	1,108	3,912
1947	9,048	3,650	8,830	1,943	1,738	4,076
1948	10,668	6,032	7,632	3,828	1,986	4,131
1949	13,187	7,223	8,740	5,106	2,228	4,264
1950	13,995	4,729	10,829	3,563	2,343	4,351
1951	33,487	4,835	8,525	3,106	2,487	4,447
1952	45,838	6,527	8,761	2,088	2,646	4,457
1953	48,594	8,936	9,448	1,978	2,834	4,554
1954	41,112	6,821	11,512	1,776	2,913	4,644
1955	38,446	6,009	12,421	2,042	3,120	4,598
1956	40,156	5,746	13,373	1,868	3,331	5,071
1957	44,017	5,947	15,734	1,775	4,209	5,538
1958	45,565	8,339	19,550	1,798	5,641	5,208
1959	45,597	8,293	20,117	1,849	6,848	6,165
1960	44,451	9,260	21,562	1,886	6,526	6,806
1961	46,995	10,375	24,980	2,090	7,245	6,248
1962	51,052	12,686	25,587	2,161	7,979	6,758
1963	50,296	14,335	27,025	2,179	9,141	7,309
1964	49,048	16,170	27,875	2,167	10,433	7,983
1965	49,443	17,825	30,285	2,177	11,121	8,380
1966	60,330	18,503	33,480	2,277	14,384	9,160
1967	71,462	19,462	40,080	2,246	15,912	9,840
1968	76,868	21,151	45,957	2,115	18,587	11,390
1969	76,272	21,189	50,563	2,055	20,346	12,853
1970	73,537	22,105	61,335	2,198	24,447	14,256
1971	70,230	25,990	72,664	2,585	29,011	13,974
1972	73,513	28,613	80,461	2,745	37,528	14,552
1973	73,534	28,654	93,187	2,631	40,574	18,202
1974	77,296	34,330	114,331	3,222	43,877	20,913
1975	84,282	40,135	145,801	3,071	54,437	23,498
1976a	88,200	45,200	159,000	3,200	60,200	27,500

Sources: Same as table A-6.
a. Preliminary.

**Table A-8. Federal Surpluses or Deficits in the Unified and
National Income Accounts Budgets, Actual and Full Employment,
Fiscal Years 1958–76**

Billions of dollars

	Unified budget		National income accounts budget	
Fiscal year	*Actual*	*At full employment*[a]	*Actual*	*At full employment*[a]
1958	−2.9	2.7	−4.5	1.1
1959	−12.9	−8.2	−5.8	−1.1
1960	0.3	7.7	2.2	9.6
1961	−3.4	9.8	−2.3	10.9
1962	−7.1	3.1	−4.0	6.2
1963	−4.8	4.6	−1.8	7.6
1964	−5.9	1.5	−2.2	5.2
1965	−1.6	1.2	1.3	4.1
1966	−3.8	−8.0	−1.1	−5.3
1967	−8.7	−13.3	−8.9	−13.5
1968	−25.2	−28.5	−12.2	−15.5
1969	3.2	−5.1	5.4	−2.9
1970	−2.8	−4.0	−0.6	−1.8
1971	−23.0	−3.9	−20.2	−1.1
1972	−23.4	−14.6	−19.5	−10.7
1973	−14.8	−10.8	−15.7	−11.7
1974	−4.7	3.1	−7.1	0.7
1975	−45.1	−11.4	−46.3	−12.6
1976	−66.5	−15.3	−59.4	−8.2

Sources: *The Budget of the United States Government, Fiscal Year 1978*, pp. 434, 437; *National Income and Product Accounts of the United States, 1929–74*. Full-employment estimates from Joseph A. Pechman, ed., *Setting National Priorities: The 1978 Budget* (Brookings Institution, 1977), table A-1, series B.

a. Calculated by assuming differences between actual national income accounts and unified budgets apply at full employment.

Table A-9. Relation of Gross National Product to Net Federal Debt, Net Interest Paid on Federal Debt, and Net Private Debt, 1916–76

Amounts in billions of dollars

Year	Net federal debt (as of June 30)		Net interest paid on federal debt (year ending June 30)		Net private debt (end of year)	
	Amount[a]	Percentage of GNP	Amount	Percentage of GNP	Amount	Percentage of GNP
1916	1.2	2.4	0.02	0.04	76.5	156
1917	2.9	4.5	0.02	0.04	82.4	128
1918	11.9	15.5	0.19	0.25	91.5	119
1919	25.0	29.3	0.60	0.71	97.2	114
1920	23.7	26.0	1.01	1.11	105.8	116
1921	23.4	32.2	0.98	1.35	106.2	146
1922	22.0	30.2	0.96	1.32	109.5	150
1923	21.8	25.5	1.04	1.21	116.3	136
1924	20.4	23.8	0.91	1.06	123.0	143
1925	19.6	21.7	0.85	0.94	132.3	147
1926	18.6	19.2	0.80	0.82	138.9	143
1927	17.4	18.2	0.75	0.79	147.6	155
1928	16.5	17.0	0.69	0.71	156.1	161
1929	15.8	15.3	0.68	0.66	161.8	156
1930	14.6	16.1	0.65	0.72	161.1	178
1931	15.7	20.6	0.60	0.79	148.4	195
1932	17.1	29.3	0.57	0.98	137.1	235
1933	19.9	35.7	0.65	1.16	127.9	229
1934	23.9	36.6	0.71	1.09	125.3	192
1935	28.4	39.2	0.77	1.06	124.5	172
1936	33.7	40.7	0.70	0.85	126.7	153
1937	35.0	38.6	0.81	0.89	126.9	140
1938	34.7	40.8	0.85	1.00	123.3	145
1939	37.5	41.3	0.84	0.93	124.3	137
1940	38.9	38.9	0.91	0.91	128.6	129
1941	44.7	35.8	0.95	0.76	139.0	111
1942	63.7	40.2	1.01	0.64	141.5	89
1943	119.2	62.1	1.50	0.78	144.3	75
1944	168.6	80.1	2.20	1.05	144.8	69
1945	212.4	100.0	3.09	1.46	140.0	66
1946	217.0	103.5	3.9	1.86	153.4	73
1947	202.0	86.8	4.2	1.80	178.3	77
1948	194.1	74.9	4.2	1.62	198.4	77
1949	194.1	75.2	4.3	1.67	208.4	81

Table A-9 (*continued*)

Year	Net federal debt (as of June 30)		Net interest paid on federal debt (year ending June 30)		Net private debt (end of year)	
	Amount[a]	Percentage of GNP	Amount	Percentage of GNP	Amount	Percentage of GNP
1950	203.3	71.0	4.4	1.54	246.4	86
1951	193.0	58.5	4.4	1.33	276.8	84
1952	193.5	55.7	4.5	1.30	300.4	87
1953	195.4	53.4	4.5	1.23	322.7	88
1954	198.5	54.2	4.6	1.26	340.0	93
1955	201.4	50.4	4.6	1.15	392.2	98
1956	196.8	46.8	4.8	1.14	427.2	102
1957	193.5	43.7	5.3	1.20	454.3	103
1958	197.2	43.9	5.4	1.20	482.4	107
1959	204.4	42.0	5.6	1.15	528.3	109
1960	204.5	40.4	6.8	1.34	566.1	112
1961	205.5	39.3	6.4	1.22	609.1	116
1962	211.4	37.5	6.4	1.14	660.1	117
1963	215.0	36.2	7.1	1.19	722.3	121
1964	214.7	33.8	7.7	1.21	789.7	124
1965	213.7	31.1	8.2	1.19	871.4	127
1966	209.6	27.8	8.7	1.16	952.1	126
1967	204.4	25.7	9.6	1.21	1,031.5	130
1968	217.0	25.0	10.5	1.21	1,147.4	132
1969	214.0	22.9	12.1	1.29	1,284.4	137
1970	217.2	22.1	13.6	1.38	1,384.9	141
1971	228.9	21.5	14.2	1.34	1,522.1	143
1972	243.6	20.8	14.1	1.20	1,716.5	147
1973	258.9	19.8	15.9	1.22	1,993.7	148
1974	255.6	18.1	19.8	1.40	2,124.9	150
1975	303.2	20.0	21.9	1.44	2,255.9	149
1976	376.4	22.2	25.8	1.52	n.a.	n.a.

Sources: Federal debt and gross national product, same as figure 7-1. Interest paid, 1916–45, calculated from Department of the Treasury data; 1946–76, *Economic Report of the President, January 1977*, p. 271, and preceding issues. Private debt, 1916–38, Bureau of the Census, *Historical Statistics of the United States, Colonial Times to 1970*, pt. 2 (GPO, 1975), p. 989; 1939–75, Bureau of Economic Analysis. Figures are rounded.

n.a. Not available.

a. Beginning with 1950, holdings of government-sponsored but privately owned agencies and certain government deposit accounts are included. The level changed from $199.9 billion to $203.3 billion.

Table A-10. Ownership of Public Debt, 1968–75

Billions of dollars

End of year	Total public debt	Debt held by U.S. government investment accounts	Debt held by Federal Reserve banks	Privately held debt						
				Total	Commercial banks	Mutual savings banks and insurance companies	Other corporations	State and local governments	Individuals	Miscellaneous
1968	358.0	76.6	52.9	228.5	66.0	12.2	14.2	24.9	75.2	36.2
1969	368.2	89.0	57.2	222.0	56.8	10.7	10.4	27.2	80.8	36.2
1970	389.2	97.1	62.1	229.9	62.7	10.5	7.3	27.8	81.2	40.5
1971	424.1	106.0	70.2	247.9	65.3	10.1	11.4	25.4	73.2	62.5
1972	449.3	116.9	69.9	262.5	67.7	10.0	9.8	28.9	73.9	72.3
1973	469.9	129.6	78.5	261.7	60.3	9.3	10.9	29.2	77.2	74.8
1974	492.7	141.2	80.5	271.0	55.6	8.6	11.0	29.2	84.9	81.6
1975	576.6	139.3	87.9	349.4	85.1	13.8	20.2	33.8	91.3	105.1

Sources: *Federal Reserve Bulletin*, vol. 61 (July 1975), and vol. 63 (February 1977).

**Table A-11. Relation of Budget Authority to Outlays,
Fiscal Years 1974, 1975, and 1976**

Billions of dollars

Description	1974	1975	1976
Budget authority available *through current action by Congress*[a]			
Appropriations	174.5	205.0	228.9
Contract authority	27.2	63.0	23.0
Authority to spend debt receipts	0.2	3.2	15.1
Reappropriations and reauthorizations	*	*	*
Budget authority available without *current action by Congress*[b]			
Appropriations	138.6	157.2	182.0
Contract authority	8.8	16.6	17.8
Authority to spend debt receipts	2.7	7.4	1.9
Deductions for offsetting receipts			
Intragovernmental transactions	−24.1	−28.9	−39.4
Proprietary receipts from the public	−14.2	−11.3	−13.9
Total budget authority for the year[c]	**313.9**	**412.1**	**415.3**
Unobligated balances and adjustments			
Unobligated balances			
Brought forward at start of year	206.9	235.6	285.7
Written off (rescinded, lapsed, and the like)	−9.6	−5.3	−15.0
Carried forward at end of year	−234.3	−288.3	−292.9
Application of new authority to prior obligations			
Budget authority of year, obligated previously	−2.6	−3.3	−4.4
Budget authority of subsequent year, obligated currently	3.4	4.4	1.9
Net obligations incurred	**277.6**	**355.3**	**390.6**
Obligated balances			
Brought forward at start of year, funded	181.8	188.3	227.4
Adjustments in expired accounts	−2.6	−0.4	−0.4
Deficiency appropriations	*	*	0.2
Carried forward at end of year	−188.4	−218.6	−251.3
Total budget outlays	**268.4**	**324.6**	**366.5**

Sources: *The Budget of the United States Government, Fiscal Year 1978, 1977, and 1976.* Figures are rounded.
* $50 million or less.
a. Enacted or recommended in the budget.
b. Permanent authorizations.
c. Through current action and without current action.

Table A-12. Budget Outlays and Budget Authority, Total and Off-Budget Federal Entities, by Function, Fiscal Year 1976

Millions of dollars

	Outlays		Authority	
Function	*Total[a]*	*Off-budget federal entities*	*Total[a]*	*Off-budget federal entities*
National defense	89,996	...	103,811	...
International affairs	4,993	−74	6,564	...
General science, space, and technology	4,370	...	4,262	...
Natural resources, environment, and energy	11,495	213	20,283	1,000
Agriculture	2,502	...	4,157	...
Commerce and transportation	18,371	1,123	20,415	−475
Community and regional development	5,393	93	5,797	89
Education, training, employment, and social services	18,167	...	21,217	...
Health	33,448	...	33,649	...
Income security	127,384	−22	140,019	...
Veterans' benefits and services	18,432	...	19,678	...
Law enforcement and justice	3,320	...	3,297	...
General government	8,790	5,863	12,318	8,946
Revenue sharing and general purpose fiscal assistance	7,119	...	9,542	...
Interest	34,589	...	34,591	...
Undistributed offsetting receipts	−14,704	...	−14,704	...
Total	373,662	7,196	424,896	9,561

Source: *The Budget of the United States Government, Fiscal Year 1978.* Figures are rounded.
a. Includes off-budget federal entities, if any.

Table A-13. Budget Surplus or Deficit, Means of Financing, and Outstanding Debt, Fiscal Years 1974, 1975, and 1976

Billions of dollars

Description	1974	1975	1976
Budget financing			
Surplus or deficit (−)			
Budget	−3.5	−43.6	−66.5
Off-budget federal entities	−2.7	−9.5	−7.2
Total	−6.1	−53.1	−73.7
Means of financing			
Other than borrowing from the public	3.1	2.3	−9.3
Decrease or increase (−) in cash and monetary assets	2.5	−0.3	−8.0
Increase or decrease (−) in liabilities for deposit fund balances, checks outstanding, etc.	−0.9	1.9	−2.0
Seigniorage on coins	0.3	0.6	0.7
Increment on gold	1.2	...	...
Borrowing from the public	−3.0	−50.9	82.9
Reclassification of securities	...	...	−0.5
Change in debt held by the public	3.0	50.9	83.4
Nonbank investors	3.2	30.9	50.9
Commercial banks	−5.6	15.6	22.8
Federal Reserve System	5.5	4.3	9.7
Outstanding debt, end of year			
Gross federal debt	486.2	544.1	631.9
Issued by Treasury	474.2	533.2	620.4
Issued by other agencies	12.0	10.9	11.4
Holders of debt			
Government agencies	140.2	147.2	151.6
The public	346.1	396.9	480.3
Federal Reserve System	80.6	85.0	94.7
Others	265.4	311.9	385.6
Debt subject to statutory limitation, end of year			
Treasury debt	473.6	532.6	619.8
Agency debt	1.5	1.6	1.7
Notes[a]	0.8	*	*
Total	476.0	534.2	621.6

Sources: Same as table A-11. Figures are rounded.

* $50 million or less.

a. Not part of the federal debt but included in the debt limit. Consists of District of Columbia stadium bonds and, in 1974 and 1975, noninterest-bearing notes issued to the International Monetary Fund.

Bibliographical Notes

Chapter 2. The Federal Budget: Concepts and Uses

Good general discussions of the unified budget are provided in the following: *The Budget of the United States Government, Fiscal Year 1969; Economic Review,* Federal Reserve Bank of Cleveland (March 1968), pp. 3–14; *Report of the President's Commission on Budget Concepts* (Government Printing Office, 1967); and President's Commission on Budget Concepts, *Staff Papers and Other Materials Reviewed by the President's Commission* (GPO, 1967). In this last volume four particularly useful papers are Ronald W. Johnson, "Evolution of Budget Concepts in the President's Message: 1923–1968," pp. 93–103; Stephen P. Taylor, "Alternative Concepts of Expenditure Timing," pp. 199–203; and two unsigned papers, "Coverage of the Budget," pp. 161–69, and "Netting and Grossing in the Federal Budget," pp. 245–61. Useful readings on federal budget concepts can be found in the May 1963 issue of *Review of Economics and Statistics* (vol. 45), which includes articles by F. M. Bator, Samuel M. Cohn, Gerhard Colm and Peter Wagner, Otto Eckstein, Richard Goode, George Jaszi, R. A. Musgrave, Carl S. Shoup, and S. Taylor, H. Wendel, and D. Brill. See also Chamber of Commerce of the United States of America, *Report of the Committee for Improving the Federal Budget* (Washington: Chamber of Commerce, 1962). On lending and the unified budget, see George F. Break, *Federal Lending and Economic Stability* (Brookings Institution, 1965). The economic implications of various budget concepts are analyzed in Wilfred Lewis, Jr., ed., *Budget Concepts for Economic Analysis* (Brookings Institution, 1968). For a discussion of tax expenditures, see *The Budget of the United States*

Government, Fiscal Year 1978, pp. 34–38; "Tax Expenditures," Special Analysis F, in *Special Analyses, Budget of the United States Government, Fiscal Year 1978,* pp. 119–42; and *Congressional Budget Office, Five-Year Budget Projections, Fiscal Years 1978–1982: Supplement on Tax Expenditures* (GPO, 1977).

A thorough explanation of the national income accounts and the federal national income budget may be found in U.S. Department of Commerce, *National Income, 1954 Edition,* A Supplement to the Survey of Current Business (GPO, 1954), pts. 2 and 3; and in Department of Commerce, *U.S. Income and Output,* A Supplement to the Survey of Current Business (GPO, 1958), chap. 2. On the full-employment budget, see *Economic Report of the President Together with the Annual Report of the Council of Economic Advisers, January 1962,* pp. 78–84; *Report of the President's Commission on Budget Concepts,* pp. 20–21; and three articles in *Studies in Price Stability and Economic Growth,* papers 6 and 7, Prepared for the Use of the Joint Economic Committee, 94:1 (GPO, 1975): Murray L. Weidenbaum, "Shortcomings in the Full Employment Budget," pp. 1–4; Nancy H. Teeters, "Current Problems in the Full Employment Concept," pp. 5–17; and Weidenbaum, "Comments on Teeters' 'Current Problems in the Full Employment Concept,' " pp. 18–19.

Good discussions of capital budgeting may be found in Maynard S. Comiez, *A Capital Budget Statement for the U.S. Government* (Brookings Institution, 1966); Gerhard Colm, "The Federal Budget and the National Economy," in *The Need for Further Budget Reform and The Federal Budget and the National Economy,* Planning Pamphlets 90 (Washington: National Planning Association, 1955), pp. 94–100; Jesse Burkhead, *Government Budgeting* (Wiley, 1956), pp. 182–211; and Richard Goode and Eugene A. Birnbaum, "Government Capital Budgets," International Monetary Fund, *Staff Papers,* vol. 5 (February 1956), pp. 23–46. A more technical discussion on the capital budget and the optimal level of the full-employment surplus is given in Martin J. Bailey, "The Optimal Full-Employment Surplus," *Journal of Political Economy,* vol. 80 (July–August 1972), pp. 649–61.

Chapter 3. The Budget Process

Information on the new congressional budget process can be found in Allen Schick, "The Congressional Budget and Impoundment Act (P.L. 93-344): A Summary of Its Provisions" (Library of Congress, Congressional Research Service, 1975; processed); and "Prepared Statement of Hon. Alice M. Rivlin," in *Five-Year Budget Projections,* Hearings before the Subcommittee on Priorities and Economy in Government of the Joint

Economic Committee, 94:1 (GPO, 1976), pp. 18–22. General discussion of the budget process, especially the executive budget process, is given in *The Budget of the United States Government, Fiscal Year 1978,* pp. 222–27. Material on recent developments in federal budgeting is to be found in congressional hearings before the House Committee on the Budget in *Fiscal Year 1977 Budget and the Economy,* 94:2 (GPO, 1976); *Zero-Base Budget Legislation,* Hearings before the Task Force on Budget Process of the House Committee on the Budget, 94:2 (GPO, 1976); *First Concurrent Resolution on the Budget, Fiscal Year 1977,* Report of the House Committee on the Budget, House Rept. 94-1030, 94:2 (GPO, 1976); and *Views and Estimates on the Congressional Budget for Fiscal Year 1977,* House Committee on Appropriations (GPO, 1976), especially pp. 58–65.

A good discussion of the politics of the budget process is given in Aaron Wildavsky, *The Politics of the Budgetary Process,* 2d ed. (Little, Brown, 1974); Ira Sharkansky, *The Politics of Taxing and Spending* (Bobbs-Merrill, 1969); and William A. Niskanen, Jr., *Bureaucracy and Representative Government* (Aldine-Atherton, 1971). Other good sources of general information are the following: Aaron Wildavsky, *Budgeting: A Comparative Theory of Budgetary Processes* (Little, Brown, 1975); Peter O. Steiner, "Public Expenditure Budgeting," in Alan S. Blinder and others, *The Economics of Public Finance* (Brookings Institution, 1974), pp. 241–342; and Joseph A. Pechman, ed., *Setting National Priorities: The 1978 Budget* (Brookings Institution, 1977).

Chapter 4. The Record: Federal Spending and Taxes

The best single source of data on the record of federal spending and taxation is the budget document itself. Every issue contains historical tables for the unified budget. Also see U.S. Bureau of the Census, *Historical Statistics of the United States, Colonial Times to 1970,* pt. 2 (GPO, 1975), Series Y 567-637, pp. 1121–24. Readable summaries of federal fiscal history are M. Slade Kendrick, *A Century and a Half of Federal Expenditures* (National Bureau of Economic Research, 1955); Arnold M. Soloway, "The Growth of Government over the Past 50 Years: An Analytical Review," and Paul B. Trescott, "Some Historical Aspects of Federal Fiscal Policy," both in *Federal Expenditure Policy for Economic Growth and Stability,* papers submitted to the Joint Economic Committee, 85:1 (GPO, 1957); and Lewis H. Kimmel, *Federal Budget and Fiscal Policy, 1789–1958* (Brookings Institution, 1959). Budget data in constant dollars can be found in Thomas J. Cuny and others, "The Budget in

Constant Dollars," Technical Staff Paper (U.S. Office of Management and Budget, 1975; processed). Details not found in any of these sources may be obtained on request from the Office of Management and Budget cr the Congressional Budget Office.

Chapter 5. Federal Budget Policy and the Economy

The relation between planned spending and GNP is discussed thoroughly in most basic economics textbooks; for example, Paul A. Samuelson, *Economics,* 10th ed. (McGraw-Hill, 1976), chaps. 11–13; Edwin Mansfield, *Economics,* 2d ed. (Norton, 1977), chaps. 10–11; and Charles L. Schultze, *National Income Analysis,* 2d ed. (Prentice-Hall, 1967).

The effects of tax or expenditure changes on the economy are also discussed in most of these same textbooks. Relevant discussions may also be found in Otto Eckstein, *Public Finance,* 3d ed. (Prentice-Hall, 1973), chap. 8; and Joseph A. Pechman, *Federal Tax Policy,* 3d ed. (Brookings Institution, 1977), chap. 2.

Discussion of the problems involved in assessing the impact of tax or expenditure changes on the economy may be found in Joergen Lotz, "Techniques of Measuring the Effects of Fiscal Policy," in Organisation for Economic Co-operation and Development, *OECD Economic Outlook,* Occasional Studies (Paris: OECD, July 1971); *The Budget and the Economy: The Outlook for Calendar Years 1976 and 1977,* Report of the Task Force on Economic Projections to the House Committee on the Budget (GPO, 1976); Committee for Economic Development, *Taxes and the Budget: A Program for Prosperity in a Free Economy* (CED, 1947); CED, *Fiscal and Monetary Policy for High Employment* (CED, 1962); Milton Friedman, "A Monetary and Fiscal Framework for Economic Stability," *American Economic Review,* vol. 38 (June 1948), pp. 245–64; and Wilfred Lewis, Jr., *Federal Fiscal Policy in the Postwar Recessions* (Brookings Institution, 1962), pp. 17–24. A more technical discussion of the subject can be found in David J. Ott and Attiat F. Ott, "Budget Balance and Equilibrium Income," *Journal of Finance,* vol. 20 (March 1965), pp. 71–77; and Alan S. Blinder and Robert M. Solow, "Analytical Foundations of Fiscal Policy," in *The Economics of Public Finance* (cited above for chapter 3), pp. 3–115.

The concept of the full-employment budget goes back to the 1947 CED publication, *Taxes and the Budget,* and to statements by Charles L. Schultze, in *Current Economic Situation and Short-run Outlook,* Hearings before the Joint Economic Committee, 86:2 (GPO, 1961), pp. 120–22, and Herbert Stein, in *January 1961 Economic Report of the President and the Economic Situation and Outlook,* Hearings before the Joint Economic

Committee, 87:1 (GPO, 1961), pp. 209 ff. See also Lewis, *Federal Fiscal Policy*, pp. 7–14. The concept was explained in *Economic Report of the President, January 1962*, pp. 78–82, and *Economic Report of the President, January 1966*, pp. 40–44. Some of the problems of interpreting the full-employment budget are discussed in Arthur M. Okun and Nancy H. Teeters, "The Full Employment Surplus Revisited," *Brookings Papers on Economic Activity, 1:1970*, pp. 77–110. For a discussion of the full-employment surplus as a measure of fiscal action, see Robert Solomon, "The Full Employment Budget Surplus as an Analytical Concept," in American Statistical Association, *1962 Proceedings of the Business and Economic Statistics Section* (Washington: n.d.), pp. 105–14. On the trade-off between unemployment and inflation, see Saul H. Hymans, "The Inflation-Unemployment Trade-Off: Theory and Experience," in Warren L. Smith and Ronald L. Teigen, eds., *Readings in Money, National Income, and Stabilization Policy*, 3d ed. (Richard D. Irwin, 1974), pp. 160–74; G. L. Perry, "The Determinants of Wage Rate Changes and the Inflation-Unemployment Trade-off for the United States," *Review of Economic Studies*, vol. 31 (October 1964), pp. 287–308; Charles L. Schultze, "Has the Phillips Curve Shifted? Some Additional Evidence," *Brookings Papers on Economic Activity, 2:1971*, pp. 452–67; William Fellner, "Phillips-type Approach or Acceleration?" *Brookings Papers on Economic Activity, 2:1971*, pp. 469–83; William Fellner, "Employment Goals and Monetary-Fiscal Overexpansion," in Phillip Cagan and others, *A New Look at Inflation: Economic Policy in the Early 1970s* (American Enterprise Institute for Public Policy Research, 1973), pp. 135–72; Robert J. Gordon, "The Recent Acceleration of Inflation and Its Lessons for the Future," *Brookings Papers on Economic Activity, 1:1970*, pp. 8–41.

Chapter 6. Fiscal Policy and the Budget Program

For general discussions of alternative budget policies, see Arthur Smithies, *The Budgetary Process in the United States* (McGraw-Hill, 1955), pp. 456–69; Committee for Economic Development, *Taxes and the Budget* and *Fiscal and Monetary Policy for High Employment* (both cited above for chapter 5); Friedman, "A Monetary and Fiscal Framework for Economic Stability" (cited above for chapter 5); and Gunnar Myrdal, "Fiscal Policy in the Business Cycle," *American Economic Review*, vol. 29 (Supplement, March 1939, *Papers and Proceedings, 1938*), pp. 183–93.

For an evaluation of the budget policy proposal of the Committee for Economic Development, see Walter W. Heller, "CED's Stabilizing Budget

Policy after Ten Years," *American Economic Review,* vol. 47 (September 1957), pp. 634–51.

Chapter 7. Fiscal Policy and the National Debt

For general discussions of the national debt, its history, its characteristics, and its economics, the following are recommended: Ansel M. Sharp and Bernard F. Sliger, *Public Finance: An Introduction to the Study of the Public Economy* (Homewood, Ill.: Dorsey Press, 1964), pp. 161–88; "Financing a Federal Deficit," Council of Economic Advisers Staff Memorandum, in *Readings in Money, National Income, and Stabilization Policy* (cited above for chapter 5), pp. 323–25; and James M. Buchanan and Richard E. Wagner, *Public Debt in a Democratic Society* (American Enterprise Institute for Public Policy Research, 1967).

For more technical treatments of the question of the burden of the debt, and also other related issues, see James M. Buchanan, *Public Principles of Public Debt* (Richard D. Irwin, 1958); Alvin H. Hansen, "The Public Debt Reconsidered: A Review Article," *Review of Economics and Statistics,* vol. 41 (November 1959), pp. 370–78; J. E. Meade, "Is the National Debt a Burden?" *Oxford Economic Papers,* vol. 10 (June 1958), pp. 163–83; Franco Modigliani, "Long-Run Implications of Alternative Fiscal Policies and the Burden of the National Debt," *Economic Journal,* vol. 71 (December 1961), pp. 730–55; E. J. Mishan, "How To Make a Burden of the Public Debt," *Journal of Political Economy,* vol. 71 (December 1963), pp. 529–42; Abba P. Lerner, "The Burden of Debt," *Review of Economics and Statistics,* vol. 43 (May 1961), pp. 139–41; William G. Bowen, Richard G. Davis, and David H. Kopf, "The Public Debt: A Burden on Future Generations?" *American Economic Review,* vol. 50 (September 1960), pp. 701–06; and Peter A. Diamond, "National Debt in a Neoclassical Growth Model," *American Economic Review,* vol. 55 (December 1965), pp. 1126–50. Many of these articles are contained in a book edited by James M. Ferguson, *Public Debt and Future Generations* (University of North Carolina Press, 1964). On the issue of the crowding out of private investment caused by deficit financing, see Keith M. Carlson and Roger W. Spencer, "Crowding Out and Its Critics," in Federal Reserve Bank of St. Louis, *Review,* vol. 57 (December 1975), pp. 2–17.

Chapter 8. Determining the Level of Federal Spending

For discussions of various proposals to share federal tax revenues with the states and localities and the criteria for allocating the financing of government programs of different levels of government, see George F. Break, *Intergovernmental Fiscal Relations in the United States* (Brookings Institution, 1967); U.S. Commission on Intergovernmental Relations, *A Report to the President* (CIR, 1955); James A. Maxwell and J. Richard Aronson, *Financing State and Local Governments,* 3d ed. (Brookings Institution, 1977); Joseph A. Pechman, "Financing State and Local Government," in American Bankers Association, *Proceedings of a Symposium on Federal Taxation* (New York: ABA, 1965) (Brookings Reprint 103); Walter W. Heller, *New Dimensions of Political Economy* (Norton, 1967); Walter W. Heller and Joseph A. Pechman, "Questions and Answers on Revenue Sharing," in *Revenue Sharing and Its Alternatives: What Future for Fiscal Federalism?* Hearings before the Subcommittee on Fiscal Policy of the Joint Economic Committee, 90:1 (GPO, 1967), pp. 111–17; and Richard P. Nathan, Charles F. Adams, Jr., and Associates, *Revenue Sharing: The Second Round* (Brookings Institution, 1977).

For a general discussion on the need for federal spending, the following are recommended: Francis M. Bator, *The Question of Government Spending* (Harper, 1960); Robert L. Heilbroner and Peter L. Bernstein, *A Primer on Government Spending* (Random House, 1963), chaps. 1–4; Roland N. McKean, *Public Spending* (McGraw-Hill, 1968); Gerhard Colm, "The Theory of Public Expenditures (1936)," chap. 2 in *Essays in Public Finance and Fiscal Policy* (New York: Oxford University Press, 1955); Walter W. Heller, "Economics and the Applied Theory of Public Expenditures," in *Federal Expenditure Policy for Economic Growth and Stability,* Papers Submitted to the Joint Economic Committee, 85:1 (GPO, 1957), pp. 98–107; and Steiner, "Public Expenditure Budgeting" (cited above for chapter 3).

For a detailed discussion of cost-benefit and cost-effectiveness analysis as applied to federal spending, see A. R. Prest and R. Turvey, "Cost-Benefit Analysis: A Survey," *Economic Journal,* vol. 75 (December 1965), pp. 683–735; Martin S. Feldstein, "Net Social Benefit Calculation and the Public Investment Decision," *Oxford Economic Papers,* vol. 16, n.s. (March 1964), pp. 114–31; Stephen A. Marglin, "The Social Rate of Discount and the Optimal Rate of Investment," *Quarterly Journal of Economics,* vol. 77 (February 1963), pp. 95–111; Charles J. Hitch, *Decision-Making for Defense* (University of California Press, 1965), pp. 43–58; Samuel B. Chase, Jr., ed., *Problems in Public Expenditure Analysis* (Brookings Institution, 1968); John V. Krutilla and Otto Eckstein, *Multiple Purpose River Development: Studies in Applied Economic Analysis* (Johns Hopkins Press for Resources for the Future, 1958); Otto Eckstein, *Water-Resource Development: The Economics of Project Eval-*

uation (Harvard University Press, 1958); Charles J. Hitch and Roland N. McKean, *The Economics of Defense in the Nuclear Age* (Harvard University Press, 1960); Robert Dorfman, ed., *Measuring Benefits of Government Investments* (Brookings Institution, 1965), especially Burton A. Weisbrod, "Preventing High School Dropouts," pp. 117–49; J. A. Seagraves, "More on the Social Rate of Discount," *Quarterly Journal of Economics,* vol. 84 (August 1970), pp. 430–50; Richard A. Musgrave, "A Cost-Benefit Analysis and the Theory of Public Finance," *Journal of Economic Literature,* vol. 7 (September 1969), pp. 797–806; and Alice M. Rivlin, *Systematic Thinking for Social Action* (Brookings Institution, 1971). Fairly complete bibliographies on the subject have been prepared by the U.S. Bureau of the Budget: "Program Analysis Techniques: A Selected Bibliography," rev. ed. (1966; processed), and "Supplement" (1967; processed), both available from the Library of the Office of Management and Budget. On the negative income tax proposal, see Christopher Green, *Negative Taxes and the Poverty Problem* (Brookings Institution, 1967); Pechman, *Federal Tax Policy* (cited above for chapter 5), chap. 4, especially pp. 77–83; and Joseph A. Pechman and P. Michael Timpane, eds., *Work Incentives and Income Guarantees: The New Jersey Negative Income Tax Experiment* (Brookings Institution, 1975).

Index

Accruals, 7, 11, 12. *See also* Revenues, federal

Administrative budget, 6

Aged, 9n, 84n, 110n, 134, 145

Allotment, 46

Apportionment, 46

Appropriations, 36–37, 41, 44

Assets, 79–80; government, 19, 20; private, 97–98

Authorization, budgetary, 5, 35–36, 37, 40, 45, 46, 49, 50, 110

Automatic budget stabilizers, 93, 94, 96–97, 103, 104, 105

Balance of payments, 83n, 85, 92, 94, 128

Bankruptcy, 125–26

Benefit-cost analysis. *See* Cost-benefit analysis

Benefit-cost ratio, 143–44

Benefits: and costs compared, 21, 138; distribution of, 18; forgone, 138; program, 138; project, 21, 137; spill-over, 136

Borrowing, federal, 19, 20, 117–26; authority for, 36; internal, 108. *See also* Debt, national

Break, George F., 7

Budget and Accounting Act of *1921*, 24

Budgetary responsibility, 131, 134–36

Budget cycle, 25; congressional role in, 38–41, 44–45; execution, 45–48; presi-

dential role, 25–27, 30–37; review of, 27, 30, 49–52

Budget, federal, 1–3, 21, 40–41; apportionment, 46; authority, 5, 35–36, 37, 40, 45, 46, 49, 50, 110; in brief, 49–50; ceiling, 45; controllability of, 52, 69–71; for current services, 25–27, 40, 50; document, 35–36, 49, 50; efficiency of, 135, 148, 149; errors in, 65–66, 68–69; fixed-cost items, 11, 13, 31, 36, 40n, 46, 55, 58, 60, 61, 68–69, 84, 96, 110n, 113, 115, 119, 125, 127, 129, 130, 131, 134, 145–46; growth of, 21, 53; intra-agency review of, 30–32; OMB review of, 27, 30, 31–32; as political issue, 2–3, 24, 31, 66, 135, 143, 147; priorities, 53, 59–62; problems, 51–52; by program, 2, 5, 9, 27, 33. *See also* Capital budget; Full-employment federal budget; National income accounts (federal budget); Unified federal budget

Budget policy, 1, 94–105; and Congress, 2, 31, 41, 89, 94, 96, 104, 145; countercyclical, 22, 96, 101–02; and deficits, 2, 21, 40, 83–85, 88–93, 97, 100, 101, 102, 103, 106–13, 115, 117–27; development of, 26; lags, 94–96; limits on, 94–98; and national debt, 2, 21, 40, 106–13, 115, 117–27; and national economy, 2, 26, 88; and OMB, 26–27, 30, 31–34; and planned spending, 79–

FEDERAL TAX POLICY
Third Edition
Joseph A. Pechman

This is a concise, nontechnical book for general readers and students interested in the use of taxation as an instrument of public policy. Thoroughly revised and updated, this edition covers the major changes made in tax laws since the last edition (1971), especially those brought about by the Tax Reform Act of 1976, and discusses problems of adjusting the income taxes for inflation and recent efforts, such as revenue sharing, to use tax policy for social purposes. The author presents and evaluates contrasting views on most taxes — personal and corporation income, general and selective consumption, payroll, estate and gift, and property taxes, as well as state and local taxes as they are affected by federal policy. This is the fifth publication in the second series of Brookings Studies of Government Finance.

406 pp./1977/cloth and paper

FINANCING STATE AND LOCAL GOVERNMENTS
Third Edition
James A. Maxwell and J. Richard Aronson

This is a lucid, nontechnical analysis of state and local finances intended to provide the educator, lawmaker, student, and voter alike with the background necessary to form intelligent opinions and make effective decisions. The diverse ways states and localities raise and spend their money, and their fiscal problems and opportunities, are examined in historical perspective.

The authors summarize current theories of the incidence of the major state and local taxes, assess the capacity of state and local governments to carry their debt burdens, and discuss property-tax "circuit breakers" and state and local retirement systems. Two chapters, rather than the one in previous editions, are devoted to intergovernmental transfers; statistical and other factual data have been brought up to date. This volume is the sixth in the second series of Brookings Studies of Government Finance.

290 pp./1977/cloth and paper